THREE FRENCH HENS,
TWO MACARONS,
AND LOVERS IN A BAKERY

A Love Story Served With Indulgent French Desserts

BY NOËLLE LOVE

Copyright 2013 Noelle Love And Little Pearl Publishing.

All Rights Reserved. Reproduction without permission is prohibited. No part of this report may be altered in any form whatsoever, electronic or mechanical -- including photocopying, recording, or by any informational storage or retrieval system without express written, dated, and signed permission from **Noelle Love**, the author, and Little Pearl Publishing. This content cannot be sold under any circumstances -- you have only personal rights to this product. This book and supplementary material was created to provide specific information regarding the subject matter covered.

All images are solely owned by the author and publisher. All rights reserved.

Recipes from the Two Macarons

Chapter 1: Mousse au Citron — 1
Chapter 2: Raspberry Macarons with Rose Buttercream — 5
Chapter 3: Fucking Blackberry Financiers — 11
Chapter 4: Tarte au Chocolat — 14
Chapter 5: Charlotte a la Framboise — 19
Chapter 6: Mille Crepes — 24
Chapter 7: Kouign Amann — 28
Chapter 8: Tarte a la Citrouille — 31
Chapter 9: Petits Pains au Chocolat — 35
Chapter 10: Chocolate Crème Fraîche Cupcakes — 39
Chapter 11: Punitions (Punishment Butter Cookies) — 44
Chapter 12: La Buche de Noel (Yule Log) — 48
Chapter 13: Croquembouche — 53
Chapter 14: Galette Des Rois — 59
Chapter 15: Cassis Macarons — 62
Chapter 16: Crepes Suzette with Orange Butter — 66
Chapter 17: Nougat Noir — 70
Chapter 18: French Apple Tart with Gold Dust — 74
Chapter 19: Tarte Tatin — 78

Chapter 20: Cream Puffs	82
Chapter 21: Gateau Basque	88
Chapter 22: Crème Brulee	92
Chapter 23: Pear Tarte Tatin	96
Chapter 24: Cherry Clafoutis	100
Chapter 25: Petit Palmiers	104
Chapter 26: Quatre-Quart Cake	106
Chapter 27: Napoleons	109
Chapter 28: Madeleines	113
Chapter 29: Chocolate Frosted Éclairs	117
Chapter 30: Chocolate Soufflé	121

1

December 22ⁿᵈ – The Eiffel Tower always looks lovely, regardless of the time of year. In spring, surrounded by the freshly opened buds decorating the nearby trees, the tower resembles a fancy ornament strategically placed by a landscape artist, handmade by someone in a foreign country so that the cost to you doubles. The hefty investment pays off, however, by the complement-filled conversations started by friends and family who travel to see it, now your pride and joy. In summer, droves of romantics disrobe at its base alongside the tourists seeking refuge under the waning shade. Ice cream vendors and souvenir peddlers collect money so easily one would think it actually grew from the metalwork. If it did, however, it is a fact that the Parisian upper-class would call it a disgrace and proceed to poison the seeds of money in the name of preserving their beloved national treasure, while, of course, pocketing a few to grow their private collection of Euros. In autumn the tower blends into the changing color palette, offering stunning photographs of its architecture robustly framed by the semi-nude branches of the maturing trees. If you're lucky, after an October rainstorm, you can catch the reflection of it beautifully complicated by the lights of Paris. And then there's winter. Freshly fallen snow blankets the surrounding sidewalks. Couples young and old bundle together, wrapped in seemingly endless pieces of material, Chanel, Lanvin, Dior, and Givenchy working together to keep the collective visitors fashionably warm, fashion trumping warmth if ever a choice had to be made. Frozen not due to the temperature but out of sheer respect of the season, the tower stands still, monstrously erect but with the decency to remain without offense, reminding all of Paris that this season, this wonderful and crazy Christmas season, is a gift, filled with enough magic to light up the world, if only you take the time to stop, look up, and notice.

This night Margot cannot help but to stop and notice the tower. Staring up at it from the window of her storefront, she gets the eerie feeling that it is leaning her direction. With one more flake of snow, she thinks, the whole damn thing could come crashing down on top of her and her bakery. It might not be the worst way to go, entertaining the idea of eminent death. The headline would read: Two Macarons Obliterated By Tower, World Mourns For Tower And Feasts On Remains Of Failing Business. Margot had finally come to terms with that idea, not the enormous tower killing her and her friends, but the fact that her business, her once booming, successful, money-making business she loved was officially a flop. Without a miracle (and who believed in those anymore?) Margot would have to close shop, leave her beloved Paris, and try to convince the next guy she seduced, if he was rich enough of course, to marry her. It wasn't the idea of monogamy that scared her (monogamy was a cinch so long as it was only a Monday through Friday type of deal), but it was the whole being dependent on someone else that made her feel nauseous. If it weren't for fucking Aubin she would be content with the idea of marrying rich and spending his money on frivolity. In fact, she probably would have almost preferred it. But over the past year and a half, ever since being convinced by that bastard to become a businesswoman, her mind had changed. She was drunk off of her newly found power and success, and would have to be dragged kicking and screaming to rehab.

"You want some?" Zenna offered Margot a spoon topped with her latest batch of mousse au citron. Sweet but with enough tartness to satisfy Margot's sour mood, Margot accepted, licking the spoon clean and then nonchalantly taking the entire bowl out Zenna's hands and plopping it snugly in her lap. Margot dangled her feet off the edge of the table, looking intently at her fiery-haired friend. She had gotten even more beautiful over the years, her light complexion lit up by the snow that reflected through the bakery's front window. No one would guess that this stunning woman once lived on the dirty backstreets of Paris, entertaining passers-by with an upturned umbrella and oversized clothes to be sure that her son would have something to eat, something that didn't come out of a dumpster, that night. Margot was proud of Zenna, persevering through a tough couple of years, saving money that she made on the street to pay her way through the prestigious pastry school, Olivier Bajard in Perpignan, nearly an eight hour ride on a train with a toddler in order to pursue what she loved – it didn't hurt that the school was well-known for the handsome, albeit aging, male faculty. The thought of Zenna losing her job if the bakery closed made Zenna feel sick again. She took another bite of the mousse and faked a smile in the direction of her friend.

From the back of the bakery, Tali emerged to catch a glimpse of the snow that was presently covering the decorated trees along the sidewalks out front. Tali was an artist, both with a paintbrush and a decorator's bag, her bright blue eyes always searching for inspiration for her next visual confection. If Tali could see herself, Margot thought, she would never need to look out another window for inspiration. Tali was extraordinarily beautiful. So beautiful, in fact, that Margot almost felt protective of her, keeping her in the back of the bakery like an evil stepmother would keep a princess locked into a high tower, away from herself so as to not feel threatened and away from men so that she could have a fair chance to get some.

But Margot wasn't threatened by Tali. It was unusual for Margot to feel threatened by anything. She wasn't a conventional beauty, she thought, her features sharp and at times almost masculine, but she was confident. It was her overwhelming confidence that attracted men to her, powerful, rich, and handsome men like Aubin, like ants to sugar. In addition to her French-conceived confidence, Margot was admired by many for her ability to dress extremely well. And being able to say that in a fashion capital like Paris is a true compliment. She always looked put-together, often wearing low cut blouses to accentuate her long, pale neck and her short, chin-length hair, which had always been curly and always blonde, regardless of the adamant wishes of her and her hairstylist. Her hair, like Margot herself, had a mind of its own.

The three French hens looked out the window of the bakery they had called home for nearly two years. Each of their gazes directed at the ominous structure that taunted them between the legs of the Eiffel Tower. The neon sign obnoxiously flashing "Delroy Doux" was enough to make Tali close the shutters of The Two Macarons. Even the beauty of the snow wasn't worth putting up with the constant reminder that in a mere three days, barring a miracle in which they would have to make months' worth of revenue in a matter of several dozen hours, all three of them would be out of a job and out on the streets. This thought, simultaneously crossing their minds like a grotesquely choreographed dance, made them synchronize their next movements, three spoons plummeting head first into what was left of the bowl of lemony mousse tucked away in Margot's Lanvin-skirted lap.

MOUSSE AU CITRON

Serves 10 (or 3-4 worried women)

INGREDIENTS

- 8 eggs
- 1 ¼ cups sugar + 1 teaspoon
- ½ teaspoon salt
- 4 lemons, for their juice and zest
- 1 cup heavy cream
- 1 ¼ teaspoons vanilla extract

DIRECTIONS

- In a saucepan, combine 4 whole eggs, 4 egg yolks (save the egg whites), and a cup of sugar; whisk to combine. Add the salt and lemon juice and zest, stirring until the mixture appears smooth. Heat the contents of the saucepan over medium heat, stirring constantly until the mixture thickens to a pudding-consistency. This should take about 10 minutes. Once done cooking the curd, strain the mixture into a large bowl, cover, and place in the refrigerator.
- In a bowl whisk together the egg whites and leftover sugar. Continue whisking until the mixture holds stiff peaks; then add to the chilled curd, folding in gently until combined.
- In a separate bowl, whisk the cream and vanilla to form peaks. Then fold this mixture into the curd. Allow the mousse to chill before serving. If in a dire state of mind, eat directly from bowl. If the mind is in a more relaxed state, divide into individual bowls and enjoy.

2

Two Years Ago - Margot stared up at the ceiling of her boyfriend's bedroom, listening to the bustle of Paris below, normal people rushing to work, pastry and coffee in hand, late as usual. She enjoyed not being normal and considered last night's revelation, that her boyfriend, Aubin, just closed a huge deal with investors in London, selling his intellectual property, and, for all she knew, a bit of his soul, for the happy sum of 7.2 million Euros, a wonderful example of it. The number boggled Margot's mind, but to Aubin, who grew up on the outskirts of Nice just minutes from the Cote d'Azur on the Guillory Estate nearly the size of Monaco itself, that deposit would just be another drop in the family's now very full bucket.

Aubin got up as usual, like a success-obsessed jockey mounted at the gate, chomping at the bit like the horse he was about to ride, eager for his next race. He pulled on his black briefs, blew Margot a half-hearted kiss from a few meters away (not bothering with the customary hand gesture – who had time for that?), and, in between brushstrokes, slurred out, "Hey babe, can you leave? I have a conference call in ten." Margot nodded and slipped on her slinky dress from the night before. On her way out the door she took Aubin in one last time, admiring his chiseled face and dirty blonde hair, not too far from her own hair's color. She had never seen Aubin work out, run, lift weights, or move with the intent of sweat at any point during their nearly eleven months together, but he had a body like a god. And, as any semi-religious girl should, that body was worshiped on a regular basis.

Below the window of Aubin's penthouse, which was on the other side of the Seine near the Champs-Elysees but far enough away from the silly Grande Roue de Paris to be taken seriously, Margot joined the herds of people below, knowing that so many of the women, like herself, were taking the ritual walk of shame, dressed in evening clothes, ridden like ponies the night before, and only slightly convinced that their male counterparts were going to call them anytime in the near future. Margot at least had the satisfaction of knowing her boyfriend was rich and that, even without a call, he would deliver what was now the customary dozen roses and the latest pair of Christian Louboutin from the designer himself who was unaware that his beautiful heels and their signature lipstick red soles had become the currency in the hiring of prostitutes for Paris's elites.

Margot rode the elevator up to her small flat in the Le Marais corner of Paris. Despite Aubin calling her building "an eyesore that even the fucking bohemians don't appreciate," she loved her home and its quirkiness. She loved the cobblestone paths, the lights that flickered on and off depending on the weather, and the artsy types that littered the stairs in front with their never ending rhymes and friendly yet intense banter. Unlike her ultra-rich boyfriend, Margot didn't come from a lot of money and she could appreciate things for more than just a luxury price tag. She always considered her family just above average, but so did eighty percent of Paris. She took after her mother, being careful about the money she spent on necessities, like living expenses and food, saving every cent she could so that each season she could buy one designer outfit. Her mother was dedicated in this endeavor and, considering the 76 years she spent committed to her closet, boasted a wardrobe that often left people, even her closest friends, under the impression that her husband made a lot of money – he did not.

Margot's father was a writer, and not a very good one at that. He was incredibly smart, and probably could have been a doctor or a lawyer or a surgeon for all she knew, but he loved to write and was stubborn enough to not let the temptation of money or success take him away from his craft. As a girl, Margot remembered listening to her father expound on his ideas for his latest novels. All of them started out great, but that was exactly the problem. None of his stories, despite their bright beginnings, had ends. When Margot asked her father why he never finished what he was working on, he would smile and say, "How am I to know where everyone is supposed to end up? I breathe life; I don't end it." He would pull Margot towards him, plant his lips on her forehead, and pretend like he was blowing out the candles on a birthday cake. "There! My daughter, live!"

She looked into her closet in her bedroom. She had a long way to go. But, looking up towards the ceiling as if to see what her mother thought, she knew that she was doing a good job of making her mom proud. She picked out her clothes for work later that day and slipped off the straps of her dress. Heading to the bathroom naked, past the hungry eyes of her little black and white cat that would have to wait just a bit longer for breakfast, Margot paused, catching a glimpse of herself in the hall mirror. Life was pretty good, she thought. Not perfect, but sensing that Aubin was going to propose to her sometime this spring, most likely on their trip to Ibiza, she felt like perfection wasn't too far away. She loved Aubin, despite his sometimes aloof behavior, and she knew that he was in love too. Getting into the bath Margot thought about the fortuitous day where she would get to tell her demeaning boss at the magazine that she quits, that she is marrying a Guillory, and that she would be taken care of in the lap of luxury for the rest of her life. Margot allowed herself to slip deeper beneath the bubbles, in no hurry to get to her job at the gossip column, hoping to hear the knock on the door from the deliveryman with her roses and shoes any minute.

Ten, twenty, twenty-five minutes passed and Margot's fingers began to look like the face of her elderly neighbor. "Time to get out," she whispered to herself, her cat now pawing at the door no longer asking, but demanding, to be fed. Margot slipped on her robe and fed her cat, which, considering her tiny paycheck and the returning fashion of exposed midriffs, would most likely eat more than Margot herself today.

Dressed in a just-above-the-knee pencil skirt and polka-dot silk blouse that buttoned down the back, Margot slipped on her heels, grabbed her phone and keys, and headed out the door for her short walk to work, nearly three hours after the majority of Paris left that morning. As she opened the door she was surprised to see a small white envelope drop to the floor. Figuring it was a message from the deliveryman and deciding she could wait until tomorrow for her latest Louboutins, Margot shoved the letter in her crowded leather purse and hurried down the stairs.

It wasn't until four that afternoon when Margot decided to check her phone for texts that she decided to open the letter out of sheer boredom. The handwriting indicated that this was not just a casual letter, but rather one of apparent urgency, scribbled hastily on the Guillory family's stationary by Aubin.

My place at five tonight – we need to talk. Can you bring food?

Wanting time to go home and change before seeing her boyfriend, Margot feigned illness and rushed home. In the mood for Indian, Margot called her favorite restaurant near Aubin's place, the aptly named India Palace, ordering more than she typically would have knowing that he would foot the bill. She then proceeded to strategically plan her outfit, each layer with its own seductive purpose, the boots to be unzipped by Aubin on the sofa, the coat to be shrugged off her shoulders upon entering, the buttons on her shirt opening one at a time coyly while they ate, and the black gilded lace romper, which with one pull of the string in the back, would gracefully fall to her ankles to the delight of her rich and handsome boyfriend's awaiting hands.

"I'm not happy," Aubin says at the sight of Margot in his foyer, hands filled with food. Thinking he was angry that she brought the food up herself rather than allowing it to be delivered Margot replied, "The delivery man was out and I thought you might be hungry sooner. I don't mind at all." Looking at his face it was clear that the food is not what Aubin was referring to. "What's wrong?" she asked, setting the bags down and touching his arm. "It's not going to work, me and you, if you don't do something that my family can be proud of. These days, women are expected to do more than dress well and stay thin. Women can run businesses and make money. Why can't you do something like that?"

Margot didn't know what to say. Aubin had never mentioned that he wasn't anything but pleased with her. Last night, in fact, while she was giving him head he sang her praises like never before. "Why do I need to make money when…" "When I have so much?" Aubin interrupted. "No, that's not what I meant," Margot said, frustrated because that is exactly what she meant. "My dad met a woman last night, two years younger than you, that opened a clothing store right beneath the Eiffel Tower. She made over a million last year. You could at least do that Margot." "But I don't know the first thing about running a business. I write a gossip column." Aubin was silent. Margot could tell that he had gotten into an argument with his father. That's the only reason for all of this business talk out of left field. Margot sat down next to Aubin who was now rubbing his temples on his leather sofa. "Don't worry about your father," she whispered into his ear. "My father?" Aubin stood up. "You think I'm saying this because of him? Fuck, Margot. When are you going to get it? I can't marry you if you're not successful. I wouldn't want to. Right now, I don't want to."

Margot felt like all of the life her father had breathed into her as a young girl left her body at once. If Aubin didn't marry her all of her plans were ruined, not to mention, she really did love him. Scared, Margot did the one thing she knew might make things better. She took off her dress herself, slid off her boyfriend's pants, and began to suck his penis. The harder she sucked the better she felt. She could figure something out. She would do anything necessary to keep Aubin and convince him that she was worthy of the Guillory name.

The next morning Margot signed the papers on a lease for a small space at the foot of the Eiffel Tower. Immediately she found Zenna, who was presently walking down a set of invisible stairs, her face painted white and her long red hair tucked away under a black hat. "I'm opening a flower shop," she announced to her friend. "Flowers?" Zenna said. "What the fuck am I going to do at a flower shop?" Of course, thought Margot, she would get Zenna to help her run the business. It would give her friend a job and give herself a perfect partner in crime, someone to bounce ideas off of, someone who could show up if she had a late night. "Did I say flower shop? I meant bakery?" Zenna's eyes lit up, apparently unconcerned about the quick change of plans from her friend. "Bakery? That I can do," Zenna smiled devilishly. "Coty," Zenna called to her son, "We're going with Aunt Margot. We're going to open a bakery."

A quick four weeks past and in that time the space Margot leased transformed into a delightful little bakery. Margot quit her job at the magazine, a few months earlier than she had planned but convinced it would help secure a ring around her finger, so totally worth it. Zenna officially finished her courses at the local pastry school, speeding up the process by several months by sleeping with one of the instructors. Her instructor gave her an "A+" on her final exam, which involved perfecting the art of filling éclairs with cream, citing that filling something with cream and taking the cream out of something, whether with your mouth, vagina, or otherwise, was pretty much the same thing.

The sign was hung out front. The Two Macarons was officially open for business. Margot opened the doors for their first day, knowing that she, like the woman Aubin spoke about a month ago who started this whole thing, was going to be successful. The universe nodded in agreement and sent a little old man by the name of Basile their way. "A raspberry macaron and an espresso," he said, unaware that he was the bakery's very first customer, but pleased to hav two attractive women helping him to what would become *his* seat at a small square table near the window. For hours he watched Margot and Zenna giggle like schoolgirls, stocking their cases with colorful macarons and discussing the extravagant wedding that was looming in Margot's, so therefore *their*, future.

The macaron, the women, the view – Basile would definitely be back. There was something special about the place and he liked it very much.

RASPBERRY MACARONS WITH ROSE BUTTERCREAM

Makes 3 Dozen Sandwiches

INGREDIENTS

- 2 cups powdered sugar
- 1 cup almond flour, sifted
- 3 large egg whites
- 2 ½ teaspoons granulated sugar
- 1/8 teaspoon salt
- Food coloring, optional
- For the filling
- 4 cups frozen raspberries
- 1 cup + 6 tablespoons granulated sugar, divided
- 2 large egg whites
- 10 tablespoons unsalted butter at room temperature, cut
- ½ teaspoon rose water

DIRECTIONS

- Prepare two baking sheets by lining them with parchment paper.

- In a large bowl, sift together the powdered

sugar and almond flour. In a separate bowl, combine the egg whites, granulated sugar, and salt, and beat with an electric mixer to form peaks. Fold this mixture into the almond mixture until just combined. Place half of the batter into a pastry bag with a plain tip and pipe onto the prepared baking sheets to create the cookies. Be sure to leave about an inch of space between each cookie, as they will spread when baked.

- If desired, you can use food coloring to dye the batter before placing into the pastry bag in order to get the colorful macaron cookies that are so popular today.
- Before placing in the oven, allow the batter to rest in cookie form at room temperature for 15 to 20 minutes. Meanwhile, preheat your oven's temperature to 375 degrees F. Place the cookies in the oven and bake for 5 minutes. Adjust your oven's temperature to 325 degrees and bake the cookies for another 10 minutes or until they appear puffed and slightly gold on top.
- Let the cookies cool on their sheets for 5 to 10 minutes before removing from the parchment paper and cooling completely on wire racks.
- To make the filling boil the raspberries and a cup of the sugar in a large saucepan, stirring to dissolve the sugar. Continue cooking the raspberries until the juice thickens and the berries themselves become soft. Strain ½ cup of the mixture into a small bowl and allow to cool. Place the remaining unstrained raspberry mixture in a separate bowl and cover to cool.
- In a heatproof mixing bowl, combine the egg whites, 6 tablespoons of sugar, and ¼ teaspoon of salt. Simmer water in a large saucepan and place the mixing bowl on top. Place a candy thermometer in the mixing bowl and cook until it reads 140 degrees F; then remove from heat. Be sure to stir the mixture often as it cooks. Once done cooking, use an electric mixer to beat the mixture until it forms a stiff meringue, about 5 minutes. Continue mixing as you add in the butter, a tablespoon or two at a time. Then add in the rose water and 3 tablespoons of the strained raspberry mixture, beating to combine until smooth. Place this mixture into a pastry bag with a plain tip.
- To assemble the macarons, spread a ½ teaspoon of unstrained jam onto the flat sides of half of the cookies. Use the pastry bag filled with the buttercream to top the remaining half of the cookies, working in a spiral from the outside in on each cookie. Press a jam-topped cookie on top of a buttercream topped cookie and gently press together. Place the finished macarons on a parchment lined baking sheet, cover, and refrigerate for several hours or overnight before serving.

3

One Year Ago - The Two Macarons was more successful than either Margot or Zenna could have imagined thanks in part to their newest best friend, and the only other employee at the bakery, Tali. Every day they opened their doors to an eager line out front. Before closing the line would reappear with tired Parisians and camera loaded tourists looking for a sweet ending to their day. The orders would clear their front cases and even dip into the reserves in the back on occasion. The only sweets left in the store by closing were the goodies Zenna reserved for her son who had become accustomed to ludicrous amounts of sugar each day. As far as Zenna could tell, however, there were no detrimental effects to the boy's health so she carried on indulging his growing sweet tooth.

More serious than the other two girls and far more practical, Tali was often the one responsible for staying late in order to fill the cases with delectable delights for the next morning. While many people would grumble about being left in the bakery alone all night, solely responsible for the business's ability to open its doors the next day, Tali enjoyed the solitude, finding it a very conducive environment for her imagination.

Margot was still in line, with so many other young women in Paris, for a proposal, but had plenty of reasons for why Aubin was making her wait. Like a true friend, Zenna helped fuel the excuses and agreed with the most outrageous, in order to keep her friend (who was now also the one who signed her paychecks) sane and pleasant. Zenna had a bad feeling about Aubin and the whole situation. She had gotten to know Aubin from different angle than Margot. And from the perspective she had, he appeared to be a womanizing dick. But Zenna kept her mouth shut. And when that wasn't possible, she kept it full.

One night, after a particularly busy day, Margot and Zenna found themselves alone in the front of the bakery, organizing the orders that they would be busy preparing well into the night. The conversation turned to Aubin and Zenna found it harder than usual to fake pleasantry. Margot hadn't heard from him in nearly a week and the excuses she was making for him were beginning to sound more insane than usual. "I just know that his car broke down after driving back from his parents'. He probably didn't want to bother them," Margot paused, "You know because they're so busy. So he didn't call and, well, he probably is walking back to Paris now." "And he hasn't called to tell you because?" Zenna probed. "Because he's going to surprise me. I'm going to be like 'Oh no! He left me.' And then, boom, proposal." Zenna turned around to take off her apron so that she could roll her eyes without offending her friend.

The small chime of the door twirled them both around from behind the counter. "Aubin!" Margot squealed. Margot was about to take off running into the arms of her boyfriend when she spied something blonde on his heels. She blinked several times hoping to un-see what she had just saw, but to no avail. There was definitely a blonde bimbo (verifiably, Margot thought, considering the fact that her mouth, which was just above a very bad, but very big boob job, was chomping away on pink bubble gum at eight o'clock on a Tuesday evening). "American," Zenna whispered. Maybe, Margot thought. A cousin? A young aunt? The woman who gave him a ride to the bakery after picking an exhausted Aubin up off the side of the road?

Margot attempted to make eye contact with Aubin, hoping to sort the whole matter out silently, but he evaded it and playfully nudged the blonde. "What do you want babe?" A capitalized "babe", a proper name "babe", Margot hoped. Zenna jumped in, observing her friend paralyzed in thought. "Two financiers Zenna," Aubin said with an inappropriate wink. "Let's get the berry ones!" Babe shouted. "A couple of *blackberry* financiers," he corrected. Zenna filled the purple bag, hoping Margot would work up the courage to say something or at least kick him in the balls, but she remained stuck in the tangled mess that was surely now her mind. Zenna handed the bag to Aubin in exchange for a handful of cash. "I don't need change," he said, handing the bag to Babe and placing his arm around her shoulder. They turned to head out the door and Zenna, not wanting to let him strut away like a cock that just left the henhouse, elbowed Margot. "Do something!" she whispered.

"What the fuck Aubin?" Margot shouted to the back of his head. Keeping his arm around Babe he stopped and turned around. "Felicia was hungry and this was the closest bakery. The food's not bad so I figured what the hell." Felicia, damn it, Margot thought, her name spoiling the idea of capital "B" Babe. "I'm sorry," Margot said directing her attention to Felicia, "but who the hell are you?" She asked the question although she knew exactly what she was going to say – "A naïve little bitch from the States who can put my legs over my head because I practice yoga every day so that your ex-boyfriend can plough me, his new girlfriend, every night." "His girlfriend," Felicia answered, leaving the rest unsaid because it was apparently too obvious to bother.

"It's over Margot," Aubin said as he was leaving. "I'm looking for something different."

FUCKING BLACKBERRY FINANCIERS

Serves 24 (lying, cheating bastards and their girlfriends)

INGREDIENTS

- ½ cup + 6 tablespoons unsalted butter
- 1 cup thinly sliced almonds
- ½ cup all-purpose flour
- 1 ½ cups + 1 tablespoon powdered sugar, and additional for finishing
- 5 large egg whites
- 2 ½ tablespoons honey
- 2 cups blackberries, fresh or frozen and thawed, cut in half

DIRECTIONS

- Preheat your oven to 375 degrees F. Prepare two 12-cup mini muffin tins by greasing and set aside.
- Over medium heat, melt the butter in a medium size saucepan. The butter should begin to simmer. Simmer for 5 to 7 minutes, scraping the bottom frequently to make sure it doesn't burn. Pour the butter and any browned pieces into a medium size bowl; cool for 5 minutes.
- Grind the almonds and flour together in a blender or food processor until fine. Pour the mixture into a medium bowl and whisk in the powdered sugar. Use an electric mixer to beat in the egg whites until the mixture is smooth. Then use a spatula to fold in the honey and browned butter. Depending on the altitude where you live you may need to add additional water or flour to get the correct consistency for the batter.
- Divide the batter between the prepared cups, about a tablespoon in each, and top with several blackberry halves. Place the tins in the preheated oven and bake for 15 minutes or until they are golden brown and springy to the touch. Allow them to cool for 10 minutes in the tins before removing. Before serving, dust with powdered sugar.

4

Meanwhile, oblivious to the blow her friend just took, Tali was in the back working on prepping the batters for several of the orders Zenna had just brought back to her. Tali loved to let her mind wander as she baked. The surprise of not knowing where it would take her was exhilarating. Some days she was transported to another time, years, decades, or even centuries in the past and other times she was catapulted into the future, given glimpses of what it held for her – a family, a loyal and kind husband, a small flat with a terrace that spanned from east to west overlooking the Seine so that she could paint both the sunrises and sunsets from the same table.

Tali was in love with Paris from the day she was born. "The City of Light," Tali whispered to herself, gazing in awe at the poster her mother kept in her bedroom tucked behind her armoire. Tali's mother was infatuated with Paris like her daughter, raising the question if a love for all things Parisian is acquired or inherited. Tali believed in the latter, considering that she had no reason to feel so strongly about a city she, or her mother, had never been to.

The poster on her mother's wall, Tali remembered, didn't always hide away in the bedroom. It used to be framed and have a prominent spot on the wall in her parent's home, which was located just outside the capital, Cardiff. The poster was relocated the day after her father died in a car accident, the night before what would have been her parents' fifteenth wedding anniversary. Her father always promised that one day he would take Tali's mother to Paris. He would dance with her in the living room to an old Lucienne Boyer record. The vinyl, warped by the sunlight that poured into the dining room, could only play one song, *Parlez-Moi D'Amour*. They would dance for hours, sometimes laughing, sometimes crying, but always smiling. In these treasured moments, Tali learned what true love was and vowed to never settle for anything less.

Heartbroken, Tali's mother threw away everything that reminded her of Paris, her husband, and the trip that would never be. The poster, purchased for her by her late husband in place of an engagement ring and placed against her window the night he proposed, was the only thing she kept. Not strong enough to throw it away but too weak to look at it and be reminded of what was lost, she tucked it away behind her wooden armoire. That spot, in the corner of her mother's bedroom, became an altar for Tali, a place to go to pray, to dream, and to talk to her dad.

Tali was only ten when her father passed away, but she knew how important Paris was to her mother and, that somewhere, hiding amidst all of the lights, was a piece of her father's heart. In a small jar in her room, Tali began collecting spare change, saving up for a train ticket that would take her and her mother to Paris some day.

But broken hearts are hard to mend and sometimes, in severe cases, are irreparable. Fifteen Euros into her savings, Tali's mother passed away. She died quietly in the hospital early one morning, Tali and her mother's sister, holding her hands as she left, anxious to be reunited with the love of her life. Tali took her fifteen Euros, the poster of Paris, and moved in with her aunt in her small, two-story stone home in the heart of Swansea. Tali's aunt was kind, but too practical to allow for any talk of dreaming, which is why Tali began to draw at age eleven. She would draw what she saw, the rundown businesses across the street, her cousin's obese cat, her mattress on the floor, until she discovered that she could close her eyes and instead draw what she saw in her own handmade world.

Considering it a favor to Tali that she had a place to live, Tali's aunt required her to do many of the household chores, including cooking for the family. Tali learned her way around the kitchen from the two cookbooks her aunt had in the kitchen, Eliza Acton's *Modern Cookery for Private Families* and *The Art of French Baking* by Ginette Mathiot. She discovered that there was a big difference between cooking and baking – you cook because you have to, you bake because you love to. Soon Tali's aunt's home filled with the decadent aromas of éclairs, soufflés, macarons, meringues, brioches, and more. The smells were so incredible that they could even overpower the stench that settled over Swansea each night, which lead to the rising popularity of both Tali and her baking.

Tali's sweets became famous throughout the city and throughout all of Wales. Proud that her niece was the toast of the town and excited to get her out of the house now that there was more blossoming than just her culinary skills - the constant advances of men, made her nervous - Tali's aunt bought her a ticket to Paris and signed her up to attend a school for those gifted in the art of pastry. Tali was thrilled to be heading to her City Of Light and to learn more about baking, but secretly she was most excited to meet fellow artists, to study their work, and to hone what had now become an obsession almost as potent as the city of Paris itself.

Baking classes at the Bellouet Conseil in Paris were challenging for Tali not because she didn't understand the concepts, she knew the techniques forwards and backwards, but because she couldn't stop her mind from seeing the world like an artist, full of color, intricate, and definitely not something that can be understood through stringent rules and narrow thinking. The star of her class, everyone, including her instructor who was particular interested in tasting the plump red lips she brought to class everyday, was shocked when Tali stopped showing up to class. A baking school dropout, Tali lied to her aunt in Wales, saying that she loved all that she was learning and how she would be eternally grateful for the opportunity. Tali didn't feel too bad because only half of that, she thought, was really a lie. She was thrilled to be in Paris, to go to the places that her mom and dad haunt, and to paint the sights of the city she grew up idolizing.

Tali painted all day and all night, selling her work for nothing so that she could afford the tiny, barely existent studio she rented above the art gallery her work was displayed in.

One Friday night the gallery hosted a large party in which much of Paris's young socialite crowd was invited. The owner of the gallery, who knew all about Tali's hidden baking talent – her son was a student in the same class at the Bellouet Conseil - asked her if she could make up a few trays of desserts to be served by waiters in black pants and ties for the night of the party. Not being able to say no to the person who sold her art and gave her a place to live, Tali graciously obliged, whipping up some of her simple classics, including one of her personal favorites, a decadent chocolate tart.

That night, after Zenna and Margot tasted the chocolate tart in front of a nude painting done by the mysterious Jacques, who Tali had yet to meet but had heard so much about (he was a bit of an urban legend in Paris – everyone aware of who he was, no one sure what he did except for the fact that he did everything), they hunted Tali down, confident that she would join them in their endeavors at their bakery next door. Zenna and Margot were shocked when they were introduced to Tali, who reluctantly answered the door of her studio upstairs. Someone who made such a devilishly dark tart couldn't be so fair and angelic. But there she was, beautiful and talented – The Two Macarons had to have her.

And have her they did because there stood Tali in the back of the bakery, daydreaming away while whipping up dozens upon dozens of the desserts that would, in a matter of hours, fly off the shelves only to be replaced by more and those replaced by more and so on and so forth forever until the day she met a man who could take her away to her flat on the Seine.

"You can leave," Margot announced as she marched into the kitchen. In all of the time Tali had worked at the bakery, never once was she asked, let alone told, to leave early. Tali wanted to ask why, but the look on Margot's face made Tali realize that it was best to say nothing at all. Tali took off her apron, placed it on the counter, and quietly made her way to the kitchen door. Zenna was nowhere to be found in the front so without any goodbyes to be made, Tali walked out the front door into the glowing dusk of Paris. She paused thinking that she heard several loud crashes coming from back in the kitchen. She briefly thought about turning back but realized that Margot was plenty capable to pick up after herself, so she continued out and into the emptying streets.

Tali looked up at the sky, about to begin a conversation with her parents, when she noticed immense clouds rolling in, blanketing the city in the down of a gray goose. A quick lap around the Eiffel tower, she thought, would give her the inspiration necessary to finish her latest landscape. Beneath the tower Tali saw a man in a bright yellow rain jacket holding an umbrella over his head, apparently caught in a rainstorm of his own. He was juggling a soccer ball with his feet, being careful not to move out from the safety of his not-in-use-but-could-be-useful red polka-dotted umbrella. That's funny, she thought, it's not raining yet, and looked at the man with the studious eye of an artist or maybe a psychologist. "You never know in Paris!" he shouted at her as she walked by, as if he heard what she was thinking. Their eyes met and she smiled. He was genuinely nice, she could tell by his toothy grin, but not the love she was looking for. She continued on her way, hoping to make it back to her place just as the rain started.

"The second most beautiful woman I have ever seen," thought Jacques as he watched her fade away into darkness.

TARTE AU CHOCOLAT

Serves 10

INGREDIENTS

- 1 ¼ cup sugar
- 6 tablespoons strong-brewed coffee, warm
- 8 tablespoons unsalted butter, at room temperature
- 1/8 teaspoon sea salt
- 4 ounces semisweet chocolate, chopped
- 2 ounces unsweetened chocolate, chopped
- 2 large brown eggs
- ¼ cup flour
- 1 teaspoon vanilla extract
- Dutch processed cocoa powder, for dusting (optional)
- For the crust
- 6 tablespoons unsalted butter, cut into tablespoon-sized squares
- 1 tablespoon canola oil
- 3 tablespoons warm water

- 1 tablespoon granulated sugar
- 1/8 teaspoon salt
- 1 ¼ cups all-purpose flour

DIRECTIONS

- Begin by setting your oven to 400 degrees F. Once hot, add together the butter, oil, water, sugar, and salt in a medium size bowl that is safe to put in the oven. Set the bowl in the oven (you should have seen that one coming) and bake for 12 to 15 minutes or until the butter bubbles and browns at the edges.

- Take the bowl out of the oven and quickly stir in the flour to form dough. Place the hot dough in a 9" tart pan that has a removable bottom. Stretch the dough a bit with a spatula and let cool. Once cool enough to touch use your hands to press the dough into the bottom and up the sides. Use a fork to prick holes in the bottom of the dough and then place in the preheated oven, baking for about 15 minutes or until it is golden in color. Allow the crust to cool completely before adding the chocolate filling.

- Set your oven's temperature to 350 degrees F. In a large saucepan, spread the sugar so that it is one even layer. Over medium heat, cook the sugar until it begins to caramelize and liquid-like around the edges. To make sure the sugar melts evenly, pull the liquid from the edges to the center of the pan. Once all of the sugar melts it should start to caramelize very quickly. Watching it closely, allow the sugar to smoke without burning. Remove the saucepan from the heat and add in the coffee.

- Stir in the butter and salt, re-heating the pan over low heat if necessary, until they melt. Then stir in the chocolates and continue stirring until smooth. Add the eggs, flour, and vanilla extract one at a time until everything is well combined.

- Pour the chocolate mixture into the prepared crust and bake in the preheated oven for about 20 minutes or until the chocolate filling begins to crack at the edges while maintaining its wiggly center. Allow the tart to cool before dusting with the cocoa powder (if using) and slicing and serving.

5

Zenna watched Tali walk out the front door from her small window view in the walk-in refrigerator. She needed a quiet place to think after seeing what just happened between Aubin and Margot; she only wished it wasn't quite so cold. Hearing the pots in the kitchen come crashing to the floor, she knew Margot would be in the kitchen for a while trying to clean up more than just one mess. Zenna stepped out of the refrigerator, feeling like a cold bitch, literally. She thought about how she may have been able to prevent seeing her best friend's heart crushed and how she unfortunately played a larger role than she would like to admit in their inevitable break-up.

The night Zenna and Margot were introduced to Tali at the gallery almost a year ago Zenna had been feeling flirtatious. She finally had enough money to buy a decent dress and the confidence she had received from that purchase as well as being a partner in a successful business had made this Parisian businesswoman's ego, and hormones, shoot through the roof. While Margot was busy trying to track down the hand that made the tart, Zenna was pulled out of the crowd and into a small room with an abstract black and white painting on the wall, lit up by a spotlight that shone from the ceiling on the other side of the room. Aubin, who was the one that brought herself and Margot to the gallery party, began discussing the underlying meaning of what to Zenna seemed to be a pretty straightforward piece of art – a large straight line with two small circles hung at the top of the canvas; on the bottom the eye was immediately drawn to a large patterned chalice. Zenna found it amusing that Aubin was not noting the obvious sexual context, but couldn't decide if it were on purpose just so that he could hear her say "penis" aloud.

Zenna glanced over her shoulder for her friend, but couldn't spot her in the spinning crowd. Were the people spinning or the room, she wondered, noting that she was on at least her fifth glass of champagne. She turned her attention back to Aubin, who had gone silent, as if in deep contemplation of the canvas before him. "It's phallic," she whispered in his ear. "Really?" Aubin grinned back. "I don't see it." "Look who I found!" Margot interrupted, dragging a man by the hand into the room. "This is my good friend and talented artist, Jacques," Margot said introducing him. "Jacques, this is my boyfriend Aubin and my best friend, Zenna. I think you two met before." Jacques shook Aubin's hand but quickly diverted his attention back to Zenna, whom he had been studying all night ever since she stepped foot into the gallery. Jacques leaned in for the customary kisses on the cheek, but stopped just before pressing his lips against Zenna's porcelain skin. "J'en peux plus," he whispered, and backed away. "Jacques wanted to show me some of his work at a gallery across town. Do you two want to come?" Margot asked. Aubin glanced at Zenna and then back to Margot, "I haven't seen much of the art here yet. I'll make sure Zenna gets home safely." Margot kissed Aubin, a thank you and farewell, and left, linking arms with Jacques, who would have walked backwards if given the chance so as to study the face he had fallen in love with just one more time.

It took Zenna a few minutes to catch her breath. What had just transpired between her and Jacques was odd. She couldn't tell if it was romantic, rude, or some mixture of the two, but she knew that whatever that was made her very horny. She knew she was in trouble. What was Margot thinking leaving her with alone with Aubin? Why would Margot leave Aubin alone with anyone? He was notoriously flirtatious and so "holy fuck" attractive that women literally stopped in their tracks to admire him, like one would study the nude body of David in Florence.

"So, Zenna," Aubin said as he moved in dangerously close, "there is really only one more piece of art I would like to take a closer look at tonight." "Well," Zenna brushed her bangs out of her almond shaped teal eyes, "let's go find it." Aubin pressed against Zenna, placing a hand on the small of her back. "I want you," he whispered.

Aubin's driver took them back to his penthouse. On the elevator ride up, Aubin strangely kept his distance, looking at Zenna like a beautiful cake, one that everyone knew was about to be opened up and devoured but that needed to be admired in the minutes leading up to that first bite. Zenna knew she looked sexy, her lace dress cut strategically to show peeks of the white skin on her breasts, and she coquettishly bit her lip as he caught her eye.

The elevator doors opened directly into the foyer of Aubin's home. Aubin turned on the lights, revealing an expansive view of the city. The fireplace flashed on in front of Zenna as Aubin took a seat on a custom-made black leather sofa. Zenna understood that he wanted her to sit down next to him, but decided it would be more fun to instigate a bit of a chase, although they both knew that in a matter of minutes they would be naked. Zenna stepped closer to the floor-to-ceiling window in the living room, looking at the buildings below.

For a brief moment she thought about where Margot was and about how she had no idea that her best friend was about to fuck her boyfriend. The guilt would have ruined the sex, so Zenna quickly distracted herself, thinking about Aubin's naked body, wondering exactly what his chest, his abs, and the goods would look like.

Zenna felt Aubin's breath on her neck as he stepped behind her. His lips, then his tongue, made their way up and down the right side of her neck, from her shoulder to her collarbone and then behind her ear. She pressed her head back towards him, letting out a sigh. His hands slipped the straps of her dress, one at a time, off her shoulders. The dress fell, stopping just before revealing her nipples. Aubin's lips moved down her back as he unzipped the dress, allowing it to fall around her ankles. His hands cupped her breasts. He squeezed her nipples and then moved his hands down her stomach and to her thong, the lace matching the dress perfectly. He played with the edge of the lace before moving in front of her and kissing her on the mouth. He directed her back to the sofa – the cold leather on her back made her tremble. Aubin stood up and undressed in front of her, a move only a very confident man would even dare. Aubin knelt down on the floor and spread Zenna's legs, using his fingers and tongue to pleasure her to the point of orgasm. Then Aubin came inside her, moving his hips slowly back and forth. He kissed her hard on the lips, grabbed a handful of her hair, and rode her until he came.

Zenna, drunk and exhausted, fell asleep on the sofa that night while Aubin moved to his room to sleep in the comfort of his own bed. At first light Aubin came back to the sofa and they screwed again. As he finished he said, "I expect you won't say a word to Margot – she'll hate you forever." Zenna had forgotten about Margot until he said her name. At that moment everything she had done became apparent, and Zenna felt sick. She went to put on her dress from last night, but couldn't because the zipper was stuck. "I don't have anything to wear to work," she told Aubin. "Can you wear this?" he said as brought out a short-sleeved black dress with a small white stripe along the bottom of the skirt. "If that's Margot's she'll know something happened." "It's not Margot's," he smiled, "just another one-time girl like you."

Zenna had been carrying around the guilt of sleeping with Aubin for months, wanting to tell her friend but too scared at the prospect of losing her forever. Now that Aubin had dumped her, Zenna had felt even worse. She knew Aubin wasn't serious about Margot and yet she kept adding wood to the fire. She had gone through wedding magazines and talked about kids, all knowing too well that Margot would never get the proposal she was so desperately sure of.

Zenna wiped the tears that had fallen off her face, replacing any feelings of sadness with anger – anger towards Aubin, but mainly towards herself. She walked into the kitchen, seeing Margot just finishing cleaning up the pots she had thrown to the floor, and decided then and there she would redeem herself by doing the one thing she knew would make Margot forgive her – making Aubin, that cheating son-of-a-bitch, pay for the heart he had broken.

"Zenna," Margot said from the other side of the kitchen, "I told Tali to leave. Will you help me with the orders for tomorrow?" Amazing, Zenna thought, she's going to act like nothing happened. Deciding going along with Margot's denial was kinder, not to mention safer, than bringing up anything to do with Aubin at the moment, Zenna smiled and took a stack of orders out of her friend's hands. "Two Raspberry Charlottes for Oralie's daughter," she said, taking out the raspberries and pear brandy to get started.

It's going to be a long night, Zenna thought, so she opened the brandy and took a swig. The brandy traveled down her throat, burning as it slipped and fell into her churning stomach. Margot also felt burnt, but rather than sit and lick her wounds she decided redemption in the form of success and lots of sex would be much sweeter.

CHARLOTTE A LA FRAMBOISE

Serves 8

INGREDIENTS

- 1 tablespoon unsalted butter, at room temperature
- 4 large eggs, separated
- ½ cup granulated sugar
- 7 tablespoons cake flour
- 1 teaspoon almond extract
- ½ teaspoon pure vanilla extract
- For the filling
- 9 cups fresh raspberries (or thawed if frozen)
- ¾ cup granulated sugar
- 1 cup water
- 1 package unflavored gelatin in ¼ cup cold water
- ¼ cup pear brandy (eau-de-vie de poire) or pear liqueur
- 2 cups heavy cream
- For the sauce
- 3 tablespoons granulated sugar, processed until superfine
- 1 ½ tablespoons freshly squeezed lemon juice
- 2 ½ tablespoons pear brandy (eau-de-vie de poire) or pear liqueur

DIRECTIONS

- Set your oven's temperature to 400 degrees F. Prepare a 9" springform pan by greasing a 9" circle of parchment paper with butter and placing in the bottom of the pan; set aside.

- In a mixing bowl, combine the egg yolks and sugar with a whisk. Add the flour, beating until smooth. Then mix in the vanilla and almond extract; set aside. In a separate bowl whisk the egg whites until they hold stiff peaks and then fold into the egg yolk mixture. Pour the batter into the prepared pan and bake for about 30 minutes or until the top turns golden brown. Allow the cake to cool.

- Prepare the filling by combining the raspberries, sugar, and water in a medium-size saucepan. Heat over medium heat until it simmers, dissolving the sugar and breaking the berries – this should take about 10 minutes. Strain the mixture over a bowl and save the puree. Place 2 cups of the puree back in the saucepan and return to low heat. The remaining puree should be saved for the sauce. Add the gelatin/water mixture to the pan and stir for 2 minutes or until dissolved. Take the saucepan off the heat and stir in the brandy; allow it to cool.

- In a large bowl whip the cream until it holds soft peaks and then fold in the cooled filling.

- Remove the cake from the pan and take off the parchment. Use a sharp serrated knife to slice the cake into 2 even layers. Place the bottom layer back into the springform pan and attach the ring. Spread the filling on top and then top with the second layer, the brown side facing up. Cover the cake with plastic wrap and refrigerate until ready to serve, no more than 24 hours.

- Before serving prepare the sauce by stirring together the reserved puree, sugar, lemon juice, and brandy. Continue stirring until all of the sugar has dissolved. Serve the cake sliced on top of a thin layer of sauce.

6

Tali woke up to the smell of wet sidewalks the next morning. The rain last night had revitalized the city and her ambition. Although she considered herself an artist who baked for a living most days, today Tali decided to embrace her baking spirit. She owed it to Margot and Zenna to really try, considering that it was their bakery that presently allowed her to paint the landscapes she really loved, not forced any longer to throw monochromatic paint blindly, splattering and spluttering all over her tiny bed, in order to appeal to the new art crowd – young people with just enough money to spend but not nearly enough to afford true art. Now with her paycheck from the bakery, she painted slowly and painted for herself. She glanced at her easel, sunlight just peeking in through her small window, and admired her unfinished work of the pool at the Jardin des Tuileries.

Tali was the first to arrive at the bakery that morning, which wasn't unusual. But today she was especially happy to have some time to herself in the kitchen. She wanted to make something special, something to tell her friends how happy she was to be one of the three "French Hens", as they were known, at The Two Macarons. Thumbing through the now tattered pages of her French baking cookbook she brought from Swansea she came across just the thing. Complex in nature, impressive on display, and delicious to the palette, a batch of Milles de Crepes cakes was going to receive Tali's undivided attention for the next several hours.

But in typical French fashion, a simple, undistracted morning can never be left alone. The door chimed and Tali, being the only soul in the bakery this morning, was forced to leave the safety of her quiet kitchen and venture out to see who Paris had brought her this morning.

Two middle-aged men in designer navy blue suits were standing in the middle of the oak floor in the corner of the bakery, looking out the window at something just beyond the Eiffel Tower. One of the men had rusty brown hair slicked to the side, most likely, she guessed, in hopes of covering a bald spot. He held an unlit cigarette between his middle and index finger, waving it up and down as he spoke to his friend. The other man, whose suit had small gray pinstripes, was wearing sunglasses, which gave Tali the impression that he too was hiding something. Despite their bad first impression, Tali looked in their direction, giving them the signal that she was there are ready to help. They must be tourists, Tali thought giving them an excuse for their odd behavior, so she put on her best smile, hoping to create impression that they were very welcome in her adopted city.

Noticing a woman behind the counter expecting an order, the men approached Tali, the one reluctantly removing his dark sunglasses. His eyes were small and beady, accentuated by his red complexion. "What can I get for you two today?" she asked. "How long have you been in business?" the cigarette asked. Thrown by being asked a question herself, Tali stammered before answering, "I guess almost two years."

"And how many employees work here?"

"Three."

The men laughed and looked at each other, seemingly relieved. "And how many customers come through here each day?"

"I don't know," Tali said, getting annoyed that they weren't ordering anything. "I'm usually in the back so I don't know."

"How much money did the bakery make last year?"

"I really don't have a clue."

Seeing that the main competition was a tiny shop run by three women, the one who they were talking to gorgeous but clearly incompetent, the mysterious men prepared to leave.

As they approached the door Tali felt it was her duty to ask them another question, especially considering how many they had just fired at her. "If you don't mind me asking, why did you need to know how much money we made last year?" If Tali weren't so pretty the men wouldn't have turned around at all. They would have walked out the door and around the corner to their parked Dacia Duster. They would have driven through the city and towards a behemoth of a building owned by their boss, France's richest man, Delroy Tasse, who would be delighted to hear the news about Paris's favorite little bakery, The Two Macarons.

But instead, Tali's pout got the best of the cigarette and he turned around. "Mon amour, if you need a job in a few months, just call me." He wrote his number down on a purple bakery bag and slid it across the counter in Tali's direction. He winked, Tali blinked, and the men disappeared.

MILLE CREPES

Serves 16

INGREDIENTS

- 4 tablespoons unsalted butter, melted and cooled + additional for the pan
- 4 large brown eggs, fresh
- 1 cup bread flour
- 1 cup whole milk
- ¼ cup pure maple syrup, grade B
- ¼ teaspoon sea salt
- For the cream
- 1 ½ cups whole milk
- 3 large brown eggs, fresh
- ½ cup pure maple syrup, grade B
- ¼ cup cornstarch
- 1 ½ tablespoons Scotch whiskey
- ½ cup whipping cream
- ¾ tablespoon confectioner's sugar
- To top
- 3 tablespoons granulated sugar
- Special tools
- A kitchen torch

DIRECTIONS

- In a blender emulsify the melted butter and eggs. Pour in the flour, milk, maple syrup and salt and continue blending until they are smooth. Allow the batter to cool overnight in the refrigerator or 6 to 8 hours.

- Set the oven's surface temperature to medium low heat and heat a 9" heavy bottomed, non-stick pan until it is hot. Coat the pan with a layer of butter, wiping out the excess with a paper towel so that there are not any pools. Carefully measure out two tablespoons of the refrigerated batter and place in the center of the hot pan. Working quickly, swirl the batter until it spreads to the size of the pan. If the crepe batter will not spread out to the sides, your pan is too hot. If this happens, remove the pan from the heat for several seconds before adding the batter and placing back on the oven top.

- You will know your crepe is ready to flip when the top of it does not look wet. Use a spatula to lift the corner and then, using your fingers to help, flip the crepe being careful not to burn yourself on the hot pan. Cook the crepe for 20 seconds on the second side, just long enough to be sure that it is cooked thorough. Place the cooked crepe on a plate (you will stack them one on top of another as you finish).

- Continue making the remaining crepes as detailed above. Don't re-butter the pan unless the crepes begin to stick when flipped. After all of the crepes have been made, keep them stacked on top of each other, but allow them to cool while you make the cream for the filling.

- Combine the milk, eggs, syrup, and cornstarch in a blender and process until smooth. Using a heavy bottomed pot, pour the blended mixture in and heat over medium low (160 degrees F if using a candy thermometer). Stir the mixture constantly until it thickens. As soon as it thickens, take the filling off the heat and add the Scotch, stirring until well combined. Allow the filling to cool.

- In a bowl beat the whipping cream with an electric mixer until fluffy. Add the confectioner's sugar in batches, beating until peaks form. Once you begin to see peaks holding be sure to stop or the fat will begin to separate out of the cream. Use a spatula to fold this into the cooled filling.

- To assemble the cake, place a crepe (be sure not to use your best one as this will be the top) on a cake plate. Spread a layer of the filling (about as thick as the crepe itself) on top. Continue stacking the layers and filling until all of the crepes have been used – don't worry if all of the filling is used; trying to used all of the filling might result in a cake that is extremely difficult to cut.

- After finishing assembling the cake place it in the refrigerator overnight (or at least 4 hours). This is important because the filling will add moisture to the crepe layers.

- Before serving the cake, sprinkle the top with the granulated sugar and use a kitchen torch to brulee it. Be sure to brulee the sugar quickly since taking too long will start to melt the filling in between the layers. Slice and enjoy immediately.

7

Margot and Zenna arrived at the bakery shortly after Tali's brief message appeared on their phones. "Men opening bakery... seem like jerks... do you know what's going on? I'm making Mille Crepes..." Their quicker than usual response let Tali know that they appreciated her baking, which made her happy, despite the disconcerting occurrence that happened just a half hour ago.

"Tali slice the cake. I have some news," Margot said as she swished by in her black pleated skirt and red strappy stilettos. Zenna followed Tali into the small office in the back, making eye contact with Margot who was leaning against the filing cabinet, her face was serious but content, reassuring Zenna that whatever the news was it couldn't be worse than the news she would have to break soon – that she had slept with Aubin and was the worst friend ever. Zenna was still plotting her revenge against the asshole. She wanted to have things taken care of before Margot found out, but she knew if she didn't act soon she would break. It would be wrong to keep such a huge secret from her friend, especially considering that Margot told her everything, every detail of her sex life, every naughty dream, every secret fantasy, and she loved that. Her friend's honesty was the attribute Zenna admired most, something she knew she could use more of in her own life. She knew the truth would be a crushing blow, but as long as Aubin was alive there was the chance that Margot could find out from someone else. The thought of that made Zenna so nervous that she had to sit down.

"Do you know who those men were?" Tali asked. "Yep," Margot answered between bites. "What did they want?" Margot, who had heard the news the night before from her good friend Jacques, smiled reassuringly. "They work for Delroy Tasse. He's opening a bakery just on the other side of the tower. He thinks he can steal all of our business." Zenna knew the name Tasse, everyone in France did; the family owned every popular business in the tourist zones; foreigners loved him and locals loathed him, although their money would say otherwise. Delroy was the heir to a fashion house, but his only passion was money. He sold his father's company for a hefty sum, invested the earnings in the shady underworld of gambling and prostitution, and then spent a very small portion of it putting local businesses out on the streets, hoping to earn the acceptance of the new generation, selling cheap products that he made, bought, procured, or stole for an even cheaper cost.

"Well, can't he?" Tali said nervously, knowing that The Two Macarons going out of business would mean her returning to painting for other people or, even worse, having to move back to Wales and settle for the fisherman her aunt had been trying to set her up with for nearly a decade.

Margot laughed, "Fuck no!" Zenna raised her fork in solidarity. "We have lines of people out our door every day. They're not just going to desert us for cheap food made by a bastard billionaire across the street. We have nothing to worry about," said Margot. "And besides," Zenna added, "if customers ever tried to cheat on us we could just put Tali out front. Ten Euros for a kiss and we'll butter your bread, buns – anything you want!" They all laughed. "My God we'd be rich!" Tali blushed, but considered it a good sign that her friends were joking about the matter.

"Well I'm glad it's nothing to worry about," Tali said as she got to work making her popular Breton Butter Cake. Zenna kidding about buttering bread made Tali crave an indulgent dessert, and nothing could ease a mind better than butter. Zenna put on her apron and began her work assisting Tali, helping where she could, but keeping a close eye on Margot, who, Zenna thought, was still at risk for a total breakdown any minute.

Margot wasn't going to lose it just yet, but she was definitely on the verge. Her hands seemed busy up front arranging the display cases for the day, but her mind was definitely not anywhere in the vicinity. The conversation she had with the other French hens seemed to go just fine, but Margot was in need of a pep talk herself. A week ago she would have been completely convinced at every confident word coming out of her mouth, but after having Aubin destroy everything that once made sense, she was unsure of everything. If Aubin could leave her so abruptly and without any remorse, couldn't her customers? Couldn't her friends?

Basile walked in, leaning on his cane and carrying a large book, his entertainment for the day, his kind voice shaking Margot from her worries. She brought him a piece of Tali's butter cake; the old man's smile lying to her saying everything was going to be just fine.

KOUIGN AMANN

Serves 10

*Basile recommends it eaten for breakfast with coffee and a nice view

INGREDIENTS

- 1 cup unsalted butter, at room temperature
- 1 cup granulated sugar
- 1 tablespoon almond extract
- 6 large egg yolks
- 2 ¾ cups flour
- ¼ teaspoon salt
- 1 large egg, broken with fork

DIRECTIONS

- Prepare a 9" tart pan by greasing the bottom and sides with extra butter; set aside.

- In a mixing bowl, combine the butter and sugar, creaming until fluffy. Add the almond extract and then the egg yolks one at a time, mixing after each is added. Continue mixing as you add the flour and salt, being sure to only mix until just combined.

- Pour the batter into the prepared tart pan and smooth with a spatula. Refrigerate the batter in the pan for 15 to 20 minutes. Meanwhile, set your oven's temperature to 350 degrees F.

- Use a pastry brush to brush the top of the refrigerated batter with the broken egg. Use a small knife to draw a cross in the center of the batter and then brush again. Place the cake in the preheated oven and bake for 50 to 55 minutes or until the sides of the cake begin to pull away from the pan. Remove the cake from the pan once you are able to handle it and allow it to cool until just warm on a wire rack. Slice and serve the cake with fresh jam or coffee.

8

Three Months Ago – Despite everyone in Paris who was under the age of twenty-five's complete and utter determination to achieve the mythical endless summer once and for all, the leaves began to change. The crisp autumn air broke the spell of summer romance and women directed their attention away from men and towards the promise of this season's perfect boots and scarves, even if it was only for a brief moment in time. The golden leaves placed a sepia film over the city's landscape, matching the color of the sunrays that bounced off the Eiffel Tower and into the eyes of the just-arriving-to-work Margot.

Margot turned the key to unlock the door to The Two Macarons, relishing the fact that she had for once beaten Tali to the bakery. Although, Margot knew, more than likely Tali would arrive in seconds, having the upstairs vantage point of seeing everyone who approached the bakery and the conscience of someone who was accustomed to hard work. Margot took a moment to herself admiring the successful business she had built and, for a split second, almost thanked Aubin for giving her the chance to know what it feels like to be independent. And then, remembering the bouncy blonde that destroyed her chance at marriage, she came to her senses, reveling in the orgasmic memories of last night courtesy of a very strong, very cute *pompier*, whose hose knew how to ignite a fire almost as well as it knew how to put one out.

"Good morning," Tali said, heading straight back to the kitchen, knowing that today, like everyday, would be busy. Only today, she thought noticing the crisp air, would require something different. In the summer customers look for sweet, in both their desserts and women, but in the fall people look to both for safety, safety from the cold and safety in a relationship, having been reminded once again of the unpleasantness of summer flings coming to an end. And Tali knew that nothing was more safe and cozy than her beloved French Pumpkin Pie.

Out front Margot readied the storefront for the onslaught of customers, placing the chairs back on the wood floor after sweeping the night before, arranging the marigolds in the vases at the center of each small table, and taking one last glance at the display cases to see if any reorganization could bring any more perfection to the rows of sugar masquerading as cakes, cupcakes, macarons, napoleons, and, her personal favorite, cream puffs. Margot almost always worked the front by herself, especially in the morning, when Zenna was running late from dropping her son Coty off at school or helping Tali in the back keep up with orders and the morning's supply and demand.

This morning was unusually slow and by the time Zenna arrived not one customer had come in. Tali came out to check which items she would need to restock, shocked to see the cases filled, not one dessert out of place, all of the rows perfectly balanced and organized. Having just set her batch of pumpkin pies in the oven, Tali found herself, for the first time in a long time, with nothing to do in the kitchen. Margot and Zenna stood at their posts behind the cash registers while Tali uncomfortably paced from the front of the bakery through the door to the kitchen and back out. At ten minutes to ten, the women were dumbfounded. Not one sale, not one customer. "What the hell is happening in Paris today?" Margot asked. Zenna shrugged her shoulders and shook her head; Tali continued pacing like a person in an asylum who just got out of her straight jacket.

At five minutes to ten Basile shuffled in, ordered his espresso, and took a seat at his corner table. Seeing Basile didn't reassure the girls that anything strange wasn't going on in the city today. Basile had come every day, literally every day, since The Two Macarons had opened. Holidays were celebrated at his corner table. Rainstorms were braved by their little old man just so that he could look out the window from his table and smile at the girls, looking up from whatever had captured his attention that day for a very brief, but very sweet, moment.

Last winter Paris had one of the worst blizzards in the history of the city. The visibility was so bad that everything closed and citizens were instructed to stay indoors for the safety of themselves and others. Tali was already at the bakery when the storm rolled through and upon hearing the news figured that she would be the only soul at The Two Macarons that day. To her surprise, from the back she heard the tiny chime of the door. The front windows looked as if they had been wrapped in white paper – she couldn't even see an inch beyond them. But there, standing with his cane and a small string around his waist, was Basile bundled up in earmuffs and a scarf around his face, ready to order his coffee.

Apparently, Tali learned, several months before the storm Basile decided to tie a small string around the handle of the bakery's door. He carried the other end of his string nearly half a mile through his front door, securing it with a small figurine of a Basset Hound he kept on his dining room table. "I knew it would come in handy one day!" Basile laughed, thrilled that he was able to find his way through the blinding storm to his favorite home away from home. Tali shook her head in disbelief, wondering if Armageddon itself would stop Basile from coming in for his daily fix.

But today there was no snow in sight, no rain falling, and, to Margot's knowledge, no fiery battles between heaven and earth raging in her city. "Something must be happening," Margot said again, this time with the intent of taking action. Enlisting Zenna to help her, Margot left her empty bakery, leaving Tali in charge of the front, to the delight of Basile, who rarely got to admire the raven-haired beauty, and to the distress of Tali, who was clearly hoping to get back to her mindless pacing.

Margot and Zenna stepped onto the cold sidewalk out front, both wishing they had worn more practical shoes instead of their fabulous, but only meant for standing or walking very short distances (like from the valet service to the restaurant's bar), over-the-knee five-inch heel boots. The streets were eerily empty, trash blowing through the air finally able to get where it was going without traffic. The girls looked at each other hoping the other had an explanation, but both remained silent. An aluminum can rolled under their heels and directed their attention to the feet of the Eiffel Tower.

"What. The. Fuck?" Zenna gasped, removing her hand from her coat pocket and intertwining fingers with Margot. "What. The. Fuck?" Margot repeated as they walked towards the beckoning tower.

TARTE A LA CITROUILLE

Serves 12

INGREDIENTS

- 1 nine-inch pie crust blind-baked and cooled (or purchase a prepared crust)
- 3 ¼ pounds pumpkin, peeled, seeds removed, and diced
- ½ cup water
- 3 lightly beaten eggs
- ½ cup brown sugar
- 4 ½ tablespoons semolina flour
- ¼ teaspoon salt
- 1 ½ teaspoons freshly grated nutmeg
- ½ teaspoon freshly ground ginger
- 2/3 cup heavy cream

DIRECTIONS

- Preheat your oven to 425 degrees F.
- Place the pumpkin in a large, heavy saucepan and cook with the water for 20 minutes to create a puree. Remove the pumpkin from the heat and allow it to cool before adding the remaining ingredients; mix well. Pour the pie filling into the prepared crust and bake for 15 minutes in the preheated oven. Lower the heat to 350 degrees F and continue baking the pie for another 30 minutes.
- Allow the pie to cool for at least 20 minutes before serving. The pie can be served warm or cold and topped with whipped cream if desired.

9

Tali brought Basile a refill of his coffee, commented on the book that he brought in today, A Man Called Intrepid (she had never heard of it – "What a pity!" he lamented), and headed back to her kitchen, leaving Basile alone at his table. Very much alone, Basile thought.

Ten years and 72 days ago Basile's beautiful wife of 51 years, Delphine, passed away. The doctors told him the cancer was terminal, but how could he believe that? How could he believe that any week the woman he shared the majority of his life with, the love of his life, the mother of his children, his best friend, was going to leave him? He made it his goal to make Delphine laugh every day after hearing the news having once heard that laughter could cure everything, even cancer. The day she died she didn't have the strength to laugh, but she smiled and held his hand, which, in Basile's mind, was even sweeter than the sound he had treasured for the past five decades.

Basile thought of Delphine every day, but lately the thought of her was more tormenting than it was comforting. His home, the one him and Delphine bought a year before she passed, was filled with so many memories of her that he couldn't stand being there alone for long. The Two Macarons had become a place for him to escape Delphine's ghost, a place for him to get lost in a book, and lost in the smiles of the three women who he, upon meeting them, nicknamed the Three French Hens. He was beyond grateful for their kindness and their store. He couldn't imagine where he would go or what he would do with himself if not for them.

"Ten years is a long time," Basile's daughter said to him one day over the phone. "Maybe you should find a friend, someone you can go to lunch with, share the rest of your life with."

"I'm 85 years old," he said, "who needs friends at my age when death is making itself comfortable in my kitchen?"

"Oh Daddy," she said. "I think it might be good for you. There are lots of women in Paris. You just need to look."

Basile hung up, intrigued and then horrified at the idea of finding a girlfriend at his age.

Despite his disliking of the idea, for the next several days Basile had thought about his daughter's suggestion. After a long inner-monologue one afternoon he came to the conclusion that the idea of a friend, one that was a woman preferably, wasn't bad in and of itself. What scared him the most was letting go of Delphine, even though he admittedly would never be over her, was replacing her smile, her laugh, her warmth with someone else's. I couldn't do that to her, Basile thought. I just couldn't. But then, he thought, what if that's what Delphine wanted? Basile imagined her looking down on him from heaven, saddened at seeing her husband alone and depressed. He knew if that he was in her position, he wouldn't want to see her suffer and wouldn't mind seeing her with another man, so long as he was a gentleman who dressed well and knew how to make her happy.

Tali emerged from the back to check on her sole customer who, she discovered, hadn't touched his coffee since she last refilled his cup nearly thirty minutes ago. "Is everything okay Basile?" she asked, sitting down on the chair across from him, resting her chin on her hand, fatigued from the boredom of the day so far. Basile looked at Tali and was reminded how pleasant having a lady's company could be. "I miss this," Basile said, surprised that he said it aloud. Taken aback by his transparency Tali joked, "What? You don't have a lady friend to bring to us?"

"My lady friend is here," he replied, pointing up towards the ceiling with his cane.

Tali understood firsthand the pain of losing a loved one and immediately empathized with him, but afraid to make them both cry with overly sentimental condolences, she decided to try to lighten the mood.

"Long distance relationships are hard," she said squeezing his hand across the table. "You might try finding a woman, strictly for the time being, a little closer. Say, Paris?" Basile was touched by her kindness and wished he were sixty years younger so that he could hold hands with Tali forever.

"Oh, I don't think so," he said, avoiding eye contact.

"Why not?"

"I don't even know what to look for anymore. The last time I asked a girl out that," he said pointing to the Eiffel Tower outside "was your age." Tali laughed.

"Well," she said standing up, "I'm sure you'll find her if it's meant to be."

A girl who believes in fate, Basile thought. That's my kind of girl.

Giving it more thought, Basile decided that he would ask a woman out, but only if Delphine gave him a sign that she approved. But what would the sign be? It would have to be something grand, he thought, something that couldn't be confused with any other of the universe's many signs. A butterfly, a rainbow, a power outage – none of those things would cut it for him.

Tali returned with a small treat, a Petits Pains au Chocolat according to the laminated sign in front of the tray in the display case, and set it down in front of him. "You need some sweet in your day," she said as she looked out the window, hoping to see her friends returning with news about the oddly slow morning they were having. With no sign of Margot, Zenna, or anyone else for that matter, Tali left Basile alone at his table for the third time that day.

Looking outside at the shimmering autumn-colored leaves outside Basile knew what his sign would be. If a woman could glow gold like that tree, he would know it was a sign from Delphine that this was a woman he could spend the rest of his time on earth with. Content with his revelation, Basile dug into his gift from Tali, enjoying every bite, his eyes focused on the door waiting for his golden woman.

PETITS PAINS AU CHOCOLAT

Serves 12

INGREDIENTS

- 2 sheets prepared puff pastry (thawed if frozen), each cut into 12 pieces (24 total)
- 1 egg, whisked
- 1 tablespoon water
- 14 ounces bittersweet chocolate, cut into 24 pieces
- Granulated sugar, for dusting

DIRECTIONS

- Preheat your oven's temperature to 400 degrees F. Prepare two baking sheets by lining with parchment paper.

- In a small bowl combine the egg and water to create a glaze. Use a pastry brush to coat the top of each piece of puff pastry with the glaze. Set a piece of chocolate on the edge of each puff pastry piece and then roll tightly to seal in the chocolate. Make sure all of the rolled puff pastry is place on the baking sheets seam side down.
- Use the pastry brush to brush the tops of each rolled puff pastry with the remaining glaze and then sprinkle with sugar. Place the baking sheets in the preheated oven and bake for 15 minutes or until they are golden in color.
- Allow the pastries to cool slightly before serving warm.

10

Margot and Zenna had seen a lot of crazy things in Paris – men tanning on the corner ass naked, Victor Victoria scenes enacted by cross-dressing prostitutes, protests, strikes, colonies of nudists on vacation, and women throwing their bras and panties at passing dark-tinted limousines just in case whoever inside was handsome, famous, or rich. Or, better yet, all three. But never in their lives had they seen anything like what their eyes set upon that fateful fall morning in front of the Eiffel Tower.

Thousands of people, businessmen, students, children, the elderly, fashion models, gay men, Japanese tourists with their cameras, and helmet-donning bicyclists, were gathered around the base of the tower. Protest was the first thing that came to mind, but considering the calm that emitted from the crowd, Margot and Zenna were forced to think otherwise. The mass of people was organized and silent, their gaze not at the steel structure looming overhead, but rather something just on the other side, just out of Margot and Zenna's view.

"What the fuck has gotten into everyone?" Zenna whispered to Margot afraid to shatter the silence and disturb the creepy crowd who at any minute, she thought, could turn whatever *this* was into a bloody riot. Margot didn't have the same feelings of fear as her friend. She was pissed that her bakery, the one thing that made her get out of her latest screw's bed, was empty. A woman on a mission, very Joan-Of-Arc in Margot's mind, she continued walking closer to the crowd, determined to discover the culprit behind whatever was diverting these normally very important people's attention away from their busy morning and away from her front counter.

Out of the corner of her eye Margot glimpsed a single solitary movement, a pear tossed in the air followed by a peach, plum, pineapple, persimmon, and a beautiful purple peony. The assorted fruit and one flower continued dancing in the air above the crowd, their movement like a small Ferris wheel for whatever bugs had thought they had found a peaceful home in the aforementioned objects. Margot tried to push her way through the crowd to find whoever it was that was juggling, apparently unaffected like them by the morning's events. And then the crowd began to move slowly, one step at a time, forward. They maintained their form, a very long line Margot realized, and stopped every few seconds because the person in front of them stopped. "It's like a fucking strung out flash mob," Zenna joked, trying to calm herself because inside she was flipping out wishing she had stayed home this morning and praying that her little Coty was fine along with the rest of Paris.

Unable to get to the juggler but recognizing him immediately through the legs of a very tall cyclist, Margot blew a kiss in his direction. The juggler, having just seen the face of the woman he was in love with, dropped his fruit on the ground and clamored to gather them all before they were juiced by the mob's slowly moving feet. Poor Jacques, Margot thought, watching him crawl on the dirty ground, expertly avoiding bicycle tires, wheelchairs, and stilettos. He wouldn't get any tips from this fucked up crowd today.

Catching a breeze, the peony avoided feet all on its own and floated over the heads of the shuffling people in the direction of Margot and Zenna. As it frolicked over Margot's head and in the vicinity of the lingering Zenna, Margot thrust her hand into the air and grabbed the dusty purple peony out of the breeze. Her foul mood unable to appreciate its beauty this morning, Margot handed it over her shoulder to Zenna. "You hold this," she said as she worked her way up towards the front of the line.

Having watched this scene unfold, Jacques, who was now perched atop one of his many unicycles, smiled and rode away.

Margot stopped mid-stride and gasped as she began to put the puzzle pieces of the mystery together. A huge sign was now visible, an obnoxiously pink flashing sign that read "Delroy Doux". The lights were flashing at the people from the top of a massive three-story building, which had apparently appeared overnight. From the top of the store was a chimney that was shooting large clouds of smoke into the air. Unlike typical factory pollution Margot was familiar with, these clouds were fluffy and white. Margot craned her neck as she watched them float up hundreds of meters over head, get caught by the breeze, and then blow into the top of the Eiffel Tower at which point the clouds burst emitting a very fine, nearly invisible powder on the people below. Margot understood -- "It's that god damn bakery!" she shouted over her shoulder to her friend.

Not hearing a response, she turned around to drag her friend up to the front of the line and demand an explanation from the first employee in her line of fire. But Zenna was no longer standing behind her. Margot twirled around to locate her friend and spotted her boots' identical twins filing themselves in line. "What are you doing?" Margot shouted as she approached Zenna, who now, like the rest of the crowd, was staring at the flashing lights waiting her turn to walk through the bakery's doors. Margot paused and, sniffing the air, picked up the unmistakable scent of Crème Fraîche. "Those bastards," Margot said aloud. "They know no one in France can resist Crème Fraîche." And apparently Zenna was one of them.

Margot tugged on her friend's sleeve, rolling her eyes thinking that Tali could make a Crème Fraîche a million times better than whatever crap Delroy Doux was mixing up in his new store. But Zenna didn't budge. Margot took a closer look at her best friend's face and froze. Zenna's eyes were no longer the vibrant green they had always been, but instead glazed over with some sort of sugary substance, turning them a horrible brown color, like the color of manila envelopes. Zenna's mouth began to open, overflowing with cream and making her look like a rabid animal. Knowing she needed to get her friend out of that line and out of the powder that was falling from the sky, Margot held her breath and grabbed Zenna's hand, jerking her out of line with the force of a car being towed out of a ravine.

Heading back to the safety of her bakery, dragging the out of commission Zenna, Margot realized that everyone was under the same spell. It was like everyone within a five-mile radius had become zombies due to whatever it was that was being released from the top of Delroy Doux's new shop. Mindlessly the people stepped forward towards their destiny, a chocolate cupcake stuffed with Crème Fraîche. Only, Margot wondered, what would happen after they got their fix? Would the city go back to normal or would they, like addicts, need more and more in order to maintain their high?

Margot pulled Zenna in through the doors of The Two Macarons, setting her down in the chair across from Basile. Tali, startled at seeing Zenna in such a bizarre state, dropped Basile's refill to the ground, shattering a white porcelain cup into hundreds of jagged pieces on the floor. Margot ignored the crashing cup, her focus intense on Zenna, who was getting worse, her skin becoming paler with each passing moment. "Is she poisoned?" Tali asked with increasing concern. Margot, desperate for a cure, straddled Zenna, climbing onto her lap and examining her face. The thought crossed her mind that she could get Zenna back in line and allow her to consume one of the cupcakes from Delroy Doux she would survive – the rest of the mob outside was. But then what? Would Zenna be a zombie forever? Would she be so hooked on the competitor's confections that she would desert her best friend?

Margot couldn't handle being dumped again, especially by the only person left that she trusted entirely, so she did the only thing she could think of. Margot leaned in towards Zenna's face and began sucking the cream out of her mouth, spitting it on the clean floor of her empty bakery. Zenna gasped for air, the life coming back to her. Margot continued by licking Zenna's eyelids clean, removing the sugary film that had sealed them shut. "Better?" Margot asked as she stood up. Zenna was about to say something, but Basile took the words right out of her mouth. "What in the hell is going on?"

As Margot began to relay the story to Zenna and Basile, Tali stepped outside and stood on top of a planter bed on the edge of the sidewalk. She saw for herself the enormous crowd of compliantly lined people, silent, moving in and out of the giant building across the way, the line wrapping around the base of the Eiffel Tower several times. She stood for nearly twenty minutes studying every aspect of the scene so that she could accurately portray it in the painting she was sure to begin that night. The line, she observed, never grew shorter. As soon as a person would leave the bakery, cupcake in hand, they would file into the back of the line, only to start the whole process over again.

Tali finished her painting several weeks later, entitling it "Le Apocalypse de Sucre," which is what all of France would come to call the strange event that began that day.

CHOCOLATE CRÈME FRAÎCHE CUPCAKES

Serves 16 (or one zombie)

INGREDIENTS

- 1 cup + 2 tablespoons all-purpose flour
- 2/3 cup cocoa powder, unsweetened
- 1 teaspoon baking powder
- 1 teaspoon salt
- ¼ teaspoon baking soda
- 14 tablespoons unsalted butter, softened and divided into tablespoon-size pieces
- 1 cup granulated sugar
- 3 large brown eggs
- 1 ¼ teaspoon pure vanilla extract
- ¾ cup crème fraîche, at room temperature + additional for serving

DIRECTIONS

- Set your oven's temperature to 350 degrees F. Prepare two 12-cup muffin pans by lining with 16 paper liners.

- Combine the flour, cocoa powder, baking powder, salt and baking soda by sifting together in a medium bowl. In a separate larger bowl, combine the butter and sugar, beating with an electric mixer until fluffy. On medium speed, beat in the eggs one at a time, mixing after each addition. Mix in the vanilla. Adjust the mixer's speed to low and beat in half of the dry mixture and then half of the crème fraîche. Mix and then repeat with the remaining ingredients.

- Divide the batter evenly between the prepared cups, making sure to only fill each 2/3 full so that they don't run over while baking. Place the cupcakes in the preheated oven and bake for 15 minutes or until a toothpick inserted into the center comes out clean.

- Allow the cupcakes to cool for 5 to 10 minutes once finished baking and then remove from the pans. Before serving, top each cupcake with a spoonful of additional crème fraîche and enjoy.

11

Three Months Ago - For the next two weeks the Apocalypse de Sucre claimed more victims, adding to the impressive line of Delroy Doux addicts, all of whom had deserted The Two Macarons, leaving the Three French hens with very little to do other than feed Basile, who managed to avoid the fiasco with a gas mask he had kept in his closet "just in case". Margot, Zenna, Tali, and Coty also remained unaffected so long as they continued to feast on their own handmade batches of Crème Fraîche each morning upon arriving at the bakery and each night before stepping out into the contaminated air. They were surviving, Margot thought one afternoon, but her business couldn't last long if their customers didn't return soon.

One night from inside the bakery Coty thought he heard a sound, a rumbling and grumbling coming from the sky. Having heard the sound themselves, the three women joined the boy in the front, staring at the monstrous rolling clouds making their way towards the city. The clouds moved quickly, pouring over the horizon like an ocean wave hitting the shore. The sky groaned again and out of its opened mouth came a tongue of lightning, striking the top of Delroy's bakery, a sign that the universe was not pleased with what was happening in its favorite city. The flash of yellow demanded the attention of the zombies below. The congregation's gaze lifted simultaneously, like a Michael Jackson music video, milliseconds before the clouds broke.

The rain poured into the eyes of all who had gathered beneath the Eiffel Tower that night, rinsing them clean and breaking the spell that had been cast nearly 336 hours ago. In an instant the victims returned to the world, free to leave and carry on with their lives, but forever affected by what took place. Delroy and his bakery had effectively created a tribe of addicts, who now, completely on their own will, would continue to return day after day for a sugar fix.

"This is crap," Zenna proclaimed, throwing her Delroy Doux cookie in the trash. It had been almost three days since the rainstorm and The Two Macarons remained vacant of customers, except for Basile and the occasional passer-by who was either too lazy to cross under the tower, too busy to wait in line, or a very small handful that were too nice to take their business away from the store they grew to love, noting that the food really was much better here than "that new bakery with all of the lights" across the street.

"Don't they realize that Delroy and his damn bakery are responsible for the two-week nightmare they were all a part of?" Margot asked.

"They don't fucking care," replied Zenna, who was busy snacking on one of the many trays of macarons left untouched after closing early yet again. "Delroy Doux is cool now," she sighed, knowing that when Parisians collectively agreed on the new "in" thing it was nearly impossible to convince them otherwise. "All their gimmicks, their flashing lights, the "Fuck-I'm-Rich Friday promotions they do giving everything away for free…"

"Their lame lounge chairs and 24-hour delivery service," Margot added.

"How the hell can we compete?" said Zenna, mouth still full.

"I don't know," said Margot, "but we have to think of something or you'll be back on the street performing and I'll have to become a professional escort." Zenna laughed, "Isn't that what you do already?"

Margot shoved Zenna playfully as they headed to the back to see if Tali, who had turned a large portion of their kitchen into an art studio recently, was busy painting her next masterpiece.

To their surprise, Tali had abandoned her paintbrush for the evening and was busy mixing something in a large glass bowl on the cement worktable Margot had "convinced" (her code for traded sex for something she wanted) a designer to create for the bakery a month ago.

"What are you making us?" Zenna asked.

"It's not for us," Tali answered without looking up from her work.

"That's rude," Margot joked, dipping her finger into the batter.

"Don't!" Tali shouted sharply, pulling Margot's finger away from her mouth and wiping it clean with a damp cloth.

"You're a crazy bitch," Margot said looking up at her friend after resigning to a seat the nearby countertop. "A little taste isn't going to hurt any of us."

Tali looked at Margot, her face suggesting otherwise. Intrigued Margot and Zenna gathered around Tali, looking over her shoulder to try to get a better look at whatever her project was.

Huddled over the bowl the three women resembled Macbeth's witches brewing over their cauldron, the toad and mutilated body parts replaced with butter, sugar, eggs, and flour.

"So what are you doing?" Margot whispered, respecting the ambience Shakespeare would have written into this scene.

"If no one else is going to punish Delroy for what he did, I'll just have to do it myself," Tali said calmly.

"What's in it?" Zenna asked, but Tali didn't respond, she just kept mixing.

Zenna and Margot left Tali alone that night, both shocked that their sweet friend had stepped into the role of evil mastermind, something both of weren't comfortable doing, at least not yet. Upon returning home they both looked up into the night sky from their bedroom windows, praying that Tali wouldn't do anything stupid. And, Zenna added, remembering the stupid things she had done in the past herself, if she did, that she didn't get caught.

PUNITIONS (PUNISHMENT BUTTER COOKIES)

Serves 12

*Tali says these cookies can also be turned into sandwiches filled with jam or chocolate for a sweeter revenge

INGREDIENTS

- 10 tablespoons salted butter, at room temperature
- ½ cup + 2 tablespoons granulated sugar
- 1 large brown egg, at room temperature
- 2 cups all-purpose flour

DIRECTIONS

- Slice the butter into tablespoon size pieces and place in a large mixing bowl. Beat the butter with an electric mixer until smooth and then add the sugar. Continue mixing until the sugar has been completely incorporated. Then add

PUNITIONS (PUNISHMENT BUTTER COOKIES)   47

the egg – keep beating until the mixture is even and smooth. Pour in the flour and stir by hand until clumpy dough forms.

- Flour a clean surface and turn out the dough. Bring the dough together into a ball and then divide in half, reshaping into balls. Cover the dough with plastic wrap and place in the refrigerator for 4 hours (or in the freezer if you're in a hurry) to firm up.

- Preheat your oven to 350 degrees F. and prepare two baking sheets by lining with parchment paper.

- Remove one dough ball from the refrigerator and place on a floured work surface. Use a rolling pin to roll the dough to ¼" thick. Take a round (or fancy if you please!) cookie cutter (an inch to 1 ½" in diameter) and cut out as many cookies as possible, placing them an inch apart on the prepared baking sheets. Scraps of dough can be gathered and re-rolled to make more cookies. When finished with one dough ball, begin with the next (or alternately keep wrapped in the refrigerator for up to 3 days).

- Place the cookies in the preheated oven and bake for about 10 minutes or until they are done but still pale in color (a little brown around the edges is just fine). Place the cookies on wire racks and cool to room temperature before dishing out your tasty punishment.

12

December 22nd (Revisited) - Margot remained in the front of the bakery, finishing licking the bowl of lemon mousse clean. Tali and Zenna had resigned to the back, desperate to come up with some incredible idea that would not only send customers clamoring back in through their front door, but one that would repair the reputation that The Two Macarons had worked so hard to create. Tali especially felt like it was her responsibility to save the bakery, considering that her previous idea had gone so horribly wrong that she cost them nearly every customer that they had gained since the aftermath of the Apocalypse de Sucre, which, Tali reminded herself for consolation, was still only a handful.

Tali had carried out her dirty deed of poisoning the head of Delroy Doux, Mr. Tasse, delivering the box of punitions to his front door herself. Unfortunately, or possibly fortunately for the Three French Hens, the amount of poison Tali put in the cookies wasn't enough to take down a man as large as Doux himself. He did, however, get violently ill, the cookies traced back to the little bakery on account of surveillance cameras that videotaped Tali arriving in addition to their signature purple box. Tali might have been brave in her plan, but looking back, she was an incredibly stupid criminal.

The French police came by The Two Macarons the day after the story of the billionaire's food poisoning hit the press, but Tali lied through her teeth, claiming that she simply was bringing the cookies as a peace offering, as a way of letting him know that there were no hard feelings despite nearly putting her and her friends out of business. Tali's nervousness resulted in tears, which helped prove her innocence in the eyes of the police, who, thankfully, were so enthralled with Tali's lips and luscious hair they had decided she couldn't be a criminal even before she opened her mouth.

Margot, who was unaware of the already conceived bias, invited the chief of police up to her apartment for "further investigation" and the next morning the bakery was cleared of wrongdoing. The chief addressed the press on the steps of the commissariat stating, "The poisoning has been ruled accidental, an unfortunate mishap that could happen to any amateur bakery of this size."

This statement, although a relief, undoubtedly angered the women – the word "amateur" perceived as a direct insult. "I fucking gave you a blow job," Margot yelled as she threw her stiletto at the television screen.

Christmas was just around the corner, which meant that revenue could, and should, skyrocket for bakeries across the world. Unfortunately, The Two Macarons was in such a slump that even the promise of a lucrative holiday didn't brighten the girls' spirits. There was no guarantee, given the current circumstances, that a single person, except of course for Basile, would walk through their doors on Christmas Eve or Christmas Day.

"How about a Yule Log display," Tali suggested, knowing that Yule Logs were very popular, very French, and for a typical bakery in a typical situation, the essential component to delightful window displays, promised to attract customers with their meringue and marzipan fashioned woodland scenes like Holly Golightly to Tiffany's after a rough night. Zenna smiled, trying to be optimistic, but knew all too well that even the most impressive Yule Logs wouldn't pay the bills. "Maybe," she trailed off, thumbing through the latest edition of French Vogue, thinking that she may never again be able to afford any of the stunning outfits, shoes, or bags pictured on the glossy pages. She looked at her Sergio Rossi black boots, reverting to her former survival mindset that got her through many cold nights, thinking how selling them would allow her to feed herself and her son for at least a month.

Looking up from her boots, Zenna saw tears beginning to well up in Tali's big blue eyes. Both her and Margot knew that Tali blamed herself for the crumbling business. Tali's guilty conscience was obvious. She showed up to the bakery everyday since the police came before dawn and stayed well into the night. Some nights it seemed like Tali even slept in the bakery, hoping that dreaming on top of the bags of sugar and flour would translate into a miraculous idea. So far, however, it only left Tali's skin even more fair and her personality almost too sweet to bear.

"I made such a horrible mistake," Tali sobbed, thinking about how naïve she was to think she could take down someone as big as Delroy Tasse without getting caught. She had barely managed to do one, and she did that poorly, running her friends' bakery even further into the ground.

"I don't think anyone has ever done anything as stupid as what I've done to you both," she said, looking up at Zenna who had come over and put her arm around her. "Oh, I'm sure people have," Zenna said, knowing all too well that she was one of those people.

"Well not you. Not Margot."

"Actually…" Zenna began, stopping mid-thought, unsure if she should divulge the secret she had kept for over a year.

Looking at Tali, understanding completely what it felt like to do something you wish you could take back, and seeing the pain in her face, Zenna knew what she had to do. Over the next ten minutes she relayed the story about the night she slept with Aubin, how there were so many opportunities for her to stop, but that she kept going even though she knew she was making a horrible mistake. Zenna thought telling someone the truth would make her feel better, like a load off her shoulders, but it made her feel absolutely horrible.

Before saying anything, Zenna could go day-to-day pretending like it never happened. She had become so accustomed to keeping her betrayal a secret that letting go of it felt more like she was losing a part of herself, not gaining freedom like so many people promise will happen.

Tali listened to the beginning of the story shocked that Zenna would act so horribly towards her best friend. But at the thought of her friend, both of her friends actually, having sex with the dashing Aubin, made her mind wander to a place it hadn't been in years. She imagined having sex with Aubin in the kitchen. Him walking in, confident like always, and without even saying a word, lifting Tali up onto the nearby counter and sliding his hands up her skirt. Tali could picture her bra being flung across the room, getting caught on the huge standing mixer in the far corner. She thought about his lips sucking hers, then her neck, and then her breasts.

The idea of sex with Aubin, no, the idea of sex in general, was unbelievably pleasant for Tali. Tali had only had sex with one person, her high school boyfriend, and they had done it three and a half times the summer before he left for an internship in London. It wasn't that Tali didn't like sex, she did, but it was as if she had just forgotten about it for the past eight years. She had been so busy keeping house for her aunt, painting, baking, thinking, that intimacy slipped to the very, very bottom of her to-do list to the dismay of the hundreds of men who thought about her every night in the privacy of their bathroom.

"So, see Tali. We all make mistakes, but we move on. It's all we can do," Zenna finished, oblivious that Tali's mind was preoccupied with Aubin's naked body. "Right?" Zenna added, surprised by her confidant's silence.

Hearing the question, Tali quickly mentally dressed herself and, trying to hide her flushed face, handed Zenna a pastry bag filled with cream, saying "yeah" as profoundly as possible. Zenna wasn't going to argue with the lack of conversation after she poured her best-kept secret out, she was still trying to figure out how she felt about the whole situation now too.

Without another word spoken Tali and Zenna got to work filling cream puffs for an order that was to be picked up tomorrow morning; Tali in reverie, Zenna in deep contemplation, both wishing they were somewhere else right now.

LA BUCHE DE NOEL (YULE LOG)

Serves 12

INGREDIENTS

- 5 tablespoons unsalted butter, melted and cooled
- ¾ cup cake flour
- 2/3 cup granulated sugar
- 4 large eggs
- Powdered sugar, for dusting
- Cocoa powder, for dusting
- Edible gold dust, for dusting (optional)
- For the chocolate ganache
- 14 ounces very dark chocolate, chopped finely
- 1 cup heavy cream
- 2 ½ tablespoons honey
- For the buttercream and syrup
- 1 cup + 3 tablespoons granulated sugar
- 4 egg whites
- 24 tablespoons unsalted butter, softened
- 2 tablespoons strong espresso
- 1 tablespoon rum
- 1 tablespoon water

DIRECTIONS

- Begin by preparing the ganache. Set the chocolate in a medium-size bowl and set aside. In a saucepan over medium-high heat, bring the cream and honey to a boil. Once boiling, pour this mixture over the chocolate and let stand for 1 to 2 minutes. Stir the mixture with a rubber spatula until it is smooth. Allow the ganache to cool at room temperature until it becomes thick, which will take 6 to 12 hours.

- Before starting to make the cake, prepare the buttercream and syrup. In a heatproof mixing bowl combine 1 cup of the sugar with the egg whites. Simmer water in the bottom of a saucepan and set the mixing bowl on top, heating the mixture until a candy thermometer reads 140 degrees F. Take the bowl off the heat and beat on high speed to cool and create stiff peaks. Add the butter and beat again until smooth. Then stir in

- the espresso until the buttercream is even in color and set aside.
- To make the syrup place the remaining 3 tablespoons of sugar, rum, and water in a saucepan over high heat. Bring the mixture to a boil, cooking until the sugar dissolves completely. Remove the mixture from heat and set aside to cool.
- Preheat your oven to 400 degrees F. Prepare a rimmed 13" x 18" baking sheet by greasing and flouring and then covering with parchment paper.
- In a mixing bowl, combine the sugar and eggs, beating on high speed for 6 to 7 minutes. Add the butter and flour by gently folding in. Pour the cake batter onto the prepared baking sheet, spreading even with a spatula. Place in the preheated oven and bake for 12 to 14 minutes or until the bottom of the cake turns golden brown.
- Spread a large clean kitchen towel (bigger than the baking sheet) on a flat work surface. Sprinkle the top with a liberal amount of powdered sugar. Turn the cake out onto the towel, remove the parchment paper, and then sprinkle again with a liberal amount of powdered sugar. Working with the shorter end of the rectangular cake, begin rolling the cake like a jelly roll, allowing the towel to be rolled into the cake. Allow it to cool to room temperature.
- After cooling, carefully unroll the cake, taking out the towel. Use a pastry brush to coat the top of the unrolled cake with the rum syrup; let stand for 2 to 3 minutes to soak in. Frost the top of the cake with the buttercream and then roll the cake up just as before, placing the seam down on a serving plate.
- Use a sharp serrated knife to carefully remove a few inches off one end of the cake, slicing at an angle (about 30 degrees). Take the removed piece of the cake and frost the flat (not angled) end with buttercream. Set this on top of the rest of the cake, creating a small stump (now you're Yule log looks like a log!). Stir the ganache and then use a spatula to spread over the cake. You can also leave the two ends of the cake and the top of the stump alone – keeping them exposed to create a more organic and unique look. Finish the Yule log by using a wooden skewer or fork tines to draw lines through the ganache so that it looks like bark. Place the finished Yule log in the refrigerator to chill and decorate as desired before serving.

13

December 23rd – The unusually bright sun pouring through the window of Margot's sixth story apartment was met with groaning and annoyance. Margot, like most bakery owners, used to love Fridays and the diversity of customers they brought through her doors – businessmen and women picking up pastries for meetings, kids coming by after school for an end of the week treat with the change they had saved from their lunch money, orders being placed by parents for weekend birthday celebrations, brides-to-be getting off work early to sample wedding cakes, and, the girls' favorite for sheer people-watching pleasure, the busloads of tourists excited to try *real* French baking. But today was different for Margot. Seeing her store empty so many times over the past several weeks, even Fridays, made her sick to her stomach. As of late, she had taken on a "why bother?" kind of attitude, tossing late bills in the recycling, ignoring phone calls from potential customers ("One person isn't going to save my bakery," she thought), and being of little to no help to Tali and Zenna who still, foolishly Margot believed, approached each day with the belief that something incredible would happen and all would be fixed forever. This morning, Margot embraced her carelessness and did as any lousy employee would – she called in sick.

Zenna's phone vibrated at the foot of the bed - *the* bed, Zenna thought, not *her* bed, which made all the difference this morning. Resting her head in the crook of the neck of her latest, and quite possibly her last, lover, she was definitely not going to be disturbed. She had never been with a man like this before, charming, handsome, talented (in more ways than one), and so obviously head-over-heels in love with her that she got the idea that she would never spend another day without him – and, surprisingly Zenna realized, she was more than okay with that; she was ecstatic.

The story of how Zenna ended up in this amazing man's bed starts last night after Tali left the bakery. Zenna had helped Tali finish up the order of cream puffs, but decided to stay longer to work on a new caramel glaze recipe she had been thinking about for the last few days, which, she decided would be the perfect finishing touch to her Croquembouche, a recipe that she loved to make but still felt like she hadn't quite gotten right even after nearly two dozen mediocre attempts.

After Tali left to embark on the short walk next-door and up the stairs, Zenna got to work, focused and determined to perfect at least one thing, besides her son, in her life. And, even her son, her pride and joy, she thought, was largely as wonderful as he was because of the help she had raising him from her parents, who looked after him several nights a week, happy to help now that she had a "respectable" job. These caramel glazed cream puffs were all her own-doing, and, if they turned out well, proof that she could still do a few things right.

Halfway through making the caramel, she began to sweat. She was nervous - nervous about her creation, about Tali telling Margot the details of her romp with Aubin, about her future, and about her son's. "You just need to focus on what you're doing," Zenna said aloud to herself, lying as she said, "If you get this right, everything will be okay."

She had the tendency in stressful situations like this to imagine that she and the universe had a special understanding and that if she made a bet with herself and won, the universe would reward her gamble. So, in the silence of the empty bakery, Tali began to take off her top. She has learned over the years (and after many, many epiphanies in men's - and one woman's - bedrooms) that she works much better when she's not distracted. And for her, clothes, especially bras, were quite the distraction. "Maybe my brain is connected to my boobs," she told Margot once after a bottle of champagne, "like a man's is connected to his penis. I can't think when my girls are being squeezed."

Taking off her shirt and bra, Zenna felt like a lizard shedding its skin, taking on a whole new persona, one free from the past and unconcerned about the future. Topless, she settled in to her work, her mind like a seashell dropped in a pool, floating slowly, back and forth, down to the bottom, gracefully arriving on the floor of fine sediment – its final resting.

Deep in focus, she shot into the air hearing the sound of the front door crashing open. A white dove flew over her head. She turned quickly to watch where it went. What. The. Hell.

"Have you seen…" a voice questioned.

"A fucking bird?" Zenna turned around, not believing her eyes.

It was Jacques.

Zenna met Jacques years ago at a party, well before their encounter at the gallery the night she left with Aubin. Margot had become acquainted with Jacques at the l'Universite Paris-Sorbonne in an acting class. The two were paired up for an improv activity that involved Margot taking the form of a wheelbarrow, Jacques a wheelbarrow-wielding farmer trying to catch a falling princess. They laughed so hard they decided that it must be good for their health to be in each other's company often, so they became friends.

Margot begged Zenna to accompany her to a party Jacques and his roommate were having, thinking that the two would make a great couple, or at least a worthwhile one-night stand. Upon seeing Jacques for the first time, Zenna was struck by his piercing blue eyes and charismatic smile, but was off put by his quirkiness. Quirky guys, she knew from experience, were complicated and too much work to get involved with. They liked to tease and she wasn't in the mood for a chase. Zenna came to the party for one reason only – a quick fuck – and she knew Jacques would take at least three maybe four dates before she got his pants off. After a brief conversation, Zenna excused herself, leaving Jacques for a muscular black-haired hunk brooding in the corner, his eyes suggesting he was just as horny as she was.

Zenna continued to study Jacques's face, shocked that he would show up in the bakery this late at night apparently chasing after a bird. It surprised her how taken she was with his good looks tonight – she had apparently never noticed just how handsome he was, always distracted in one way or another. Those eyes, she thought, were the kindest most honest eyes she had ever seen. His nose was strong, sharp but not overtly, and his mouth was… wide open.

Remembering she was topless, she understood the stunned look on Jacques's face, something like a boy who just got told he could go on a water slide for the first time, thrilled but nervous at the size and, in this case, large nipples. Zenna scoured her brain for something witty to say to explain why her breasts were having a night out, but before she could decide on which "Girls Just Want To Have Fun" reference to use, Jacques ran out the door and into the cold dark night.

Something came over Zenna and she knew that she couldn't let Jacques run off. She needed to look at his face more; she needed to touch him. Sprinting into the streets of Paris Zenna looked frantically for the back of Jacques's head. At this time of night under the Eiffel Tower spotting a single person was easy, considering that every other shadow was two-headed with wandering hands. Zenna stood on a bench nearby to improve her view and found her single headed man walking towards the base of the sparkling tower. Smiling, Zenna ran through the couples towards Jacques. The gasps and whispers coming from several people behind him alerted Jacques to Zenna's presence. He stopped and turned around, head down, staring at his feet.

"When a girl bears her breasts for you the least you can say is hi." Zenna put her hands on her hips, catching her breath and waiting for Jacques's response. His smile was enough to send Zenna sailing over the moon. Still studying his shoes, afraid to look anywhere above her ankles, Jacques boyishly said hi.

"You can look. Everyone else is," she laughed.

Knowing this was his one shot to make a good impression, Jacques lifted his gaze to make eye contact, exerting as much self-control as was humanly possible to prevent his stare stopping halfway up and admiring her perfect boobs.

Zenna's half-nude presence in the middle of the plaza had rightfully attracted quite a crowd, which, until this moment, had been non-existent to the two. Looking around at the stunned faces, they both laughed at the situation.

"Now what?" Jacques shrugged. Zenna turned up a corner of her mouth, playfully moving her shoulders up and down towards her ears.

"This," Jacques thought, "is the girl for me." "Here goes nothing!" he whispered into her ear, proceeding to take off his pants and boxers, leaving his socks on for full effect.

Zenna couldn't believe what Jacques had just done and laughed uncontrollably.

"I hope you're not laughing at me," he said looking down at his penis. "It's pretty cold out here."

Zenna laughed one more time and then placed her hand in his. "In that case," she said, "let's get you somewhere warm."

The flapping of wings drew the couple's attention upward to the dove flying over their heads. The bird was headed towards a small flat perched on a hill. It was adorned with twinkle lights and the view, Zenna realized, must frame The Two Macarons perfectly beneath the legs of the Eiffel Tower. Zenna squeezed Jacques's hand harder; he returned the gesture. Like two small kids who had fallen in love at recess, Jacques and Zenna leisurely strolled towards the beaconing home, both knowing that the bed would be their first and last stop that night. They were very aware of the stares being shot at them from all directions, but already much too in love with each other to care.

CROQUEMBOUCHE

Serves 30

INGREDIENTS

- ½ cup whole milk
- ½ cup lukewarm water
- 8 tablespoons unsalted butter
- 1 teaspoon kosher salt

- 1 cup all-purpose flour
- 5 large eggs
- 1 egg yolk
- ½ cup heavy cream
- For the caramel cream
- 1 ½ cups granulated sugar
- ¼ cup water
- 2 cups heavy cream
- ¼ cup crème fraîche
- ½ teaspoon vanilla extract
- 1/8 teaspoon kosher salt
- For the caramel
- 1 cup granulated sugar
- 2 ½ tablespoons water
- ¾ teaspoon freshly squeezed lemon juice

DIRECTIONS

- After creating an ice water bath in the sink and setting a bowl in the center, start the process of making the caramel cream. In a medium size saucepan combine the sugar and water. Heat the saucepan over medium-high heat and bring to a boil to dissolve the sugar. Lower the heat to medium and cook for another 5 minutes or until the mixture turns dark in color. Quickly remove it from the heat, add in half of the heavy cream, and whisk. Place the saucepan back over medium heat and bring to a boil again.

- Once boiling, pour the sugar mixture (which is hopefully now caramel!) into the prepared ice water bath. Stir it as it cools for 10 to 12 minutes. Add in the crème fraîche, vanilla, and salt, stirring to combine. Cover the bowl with plastic wrap and place in the refrigerator for up to 2 hours (or up to 5 days) before using.

- Set your oven's temperature to 400 degrees F. Prepare two baking sheets by lining with parchment paper and set aside.

- To prepare the cream puffs, combine the milk, water, butter, and salt in a medium-size saucepan. Heat the saucepan over medium-high heat, bringing the mixture to a boil. Take the saucepan off the heat and add the flour, whisking to combine. Place the saucepan back over the heat and cook for 4 to 5 minutes, stirring constantly. When finished the mixture should start to pull away from the sides of the saucepan. Pour the mixture into a mixing bowl and beat with an electric mixer for 1 minute on medium speed.

- Continue beating as you add the eggs (not the single egg yolk) one at a time, mixing after each one is added. Use a spatula to transfer the dough into a pastry bag with a round tip. Use the bag to pipe the cream puffs into quarter-sized mounds on the prepared baking sheets.

- In a clean mixing bowl, combine the egg yolk and heavy cream with a whisk. Brush the egg wash over the tops of the cream puff dough. Set the baking sheets in the preheated oven and bake for about 22 minutes or until the tops begin to turn golden brown. Allow the puffs to cool on the baking sheets set on top of cooling racks.

- Once the puffs cool, place the remaining cup of heavy cream from the caramel cream recipe in a mixing bowl and beat with an electric mixer until it holds stiff peaks. Take the cooled caramel out of the refrigerator and fold in the whipped cream. Use a whisk if necessary to thicken the mixture, whisking for a minute or two. Transfer the caramel cream into a pastry bag with round tip. Place the tip into the bottom of each cream puff and fill, setting the cream puffs back on the baking sheets as you finish.

- When you are ready to assemble the Croquembouche, prepare the caramel by creating another ice-water bath in the sink. Place all of the caramel ingredients in a small saucepan and heat over medium heat. Allow the caramel to cook for 5 minutes so that the sugar dissolves – don't stir as it cooks. Adjust the heat to high and cook the caramel for another 5 minutes or until it is dark in color. Every minute or so swirl the pan to make sure the caramel cooks evenly. Take the caramel off the heat and place the bottom of the saucepan in the ice water to stop the cooking – this just takes a few seconds.

- Take a filled cream puff and dip the bottom half into the hot caramel. Set the dipped cream puff on a serving platter, caramel side down. Continue dipping cream puffs into the caramel, creating a ring of 10 on the platter and then stacking additional cream puffs on top to form a layered-pyramid (5 to 6 layers will use about 40 to 50 cream puffs). If you need to reheat the caramel to keep dipping, reheat for a few minutes over low heat. Any extra caramel can be drizzled over the top of the pyramid.

- Your finished Croquembouche makes a beautiful centerpiece for holiday parties and is an instant crowd-pleaser at dinners. Your creation can be at room temperature for 2 hours before eating.

14

Tali opened the bakery that day for her two friends, both of whom had called her just minutes ago saying that they weren't going to be in this morning. Tali opened the bakery's shutters and breathed heavily on the glass window, drawing a small heart in the fog. After studying the small heart for a moment, she waved her hand over it and made it disappear, realizing it was very uncharacteristic for her to have done such a thing.

Tali had always been the type of girl very content to be alone. In fact she preferred it, which is why when given the chance to live with Margot in her flat a few blocks away or a studio that was just big enough for her to lie down flat in both directions above the art gallery she chose the latter. She enjoyed Margot and found her to be incredibly interesting (as well as the subject for many of her sketches citing her unique features as "irresistible") but couldn't fathom the idea of living with someone so exuberant and outgoing. Tali knew that there would always be people at Margot's, parties, impromptu gatherings, and she would be forced to socialize as the roommate.

Tali wasn't what you would consider anti-social though. She loved people, so long as they had the tendency of being quiet and were serious enough to appreciate a good book even in light of an invitation to a raucous party. Most people who knew Tali in high school would wager that ten years after graduation she would be working as a librarian (but maybe that is just what they fantasized about). Tali's looks had given her the opportunity to be incredibly popular, but her reserved personality kept her out of the "cool" crowd even as an adult.

But something in the air today was making Tali feeling romantic, which is what prompted her to draw the small heart in the first place. Last night she couldn't sleep, very aware and strangely upset that she was alone. After fantasizing about having sex with Aubin she couldn't get the idea out of her mind. Everything turned her on in the past twelve hours, filling the cream puffs, the erect Eiffel Tower standing outside her tight apartment, even, she hated to admit, her electric toothbrush. She was embarrassed when she thought about how long ago was the last time she had sex, almost eight years, with her one and only boyfriend, a successful banker now living with his Italian wife and twins (daughters not prostitutes) in Zurich.

Tali began setting out the morning pastries, fully aware that it was busy work considering that chances were the only person walking through the door of The Two Macarons today was Basile. She hoped that the work would clear her mind of her rediscovered sexuality, but it was too menial to distract her from the vivid erotica that was taking place in her mind. Thankfully, Basile walked in shortly after, giving Tali momentary relief. It would be Basile's usual this morning, espresso and macaron. After making sure he settled into his spot and decided which table to place their one bouquet of flowers on this morning (by the window to lure customers in or, at least she thought, so it could be appreciated by those who passed by), Tali headed back to the kitchen, determined to work on the apricot filled Galette Des Rois she was planning on giving Basile as a Christmas gift, hoping that baking would be the solution to eradicating her naughtiness.

GALETTE DES ROIS

Serves 6

INGREDIENTS

- 14 ounces prepared puff pastry
- 2 ½ tablespoons apricot jam
- 6 ½ tablespoons butter, softened
- 6 tablespoons granulated sugar, processed until very fine
- 2 eggs, whisked (divided in half)
- 6 tablespoons ground almonds
- 2 tablespoons dark rum

DIRECTIONS

- Preheat your oven to 400 degrees F.
- Separate the puff pastry into two equal halves and roll into 10" rounds. Place one round on a baking sheet and spread the apricot jam on top in an even layer, leaving a bit of a border around the edges.

- In a small mixing bowl combine the butter and sugar and mix until fluffy. Continue mixing as you add in one of the whisked eggs. Use a spatula to stir in the almonds and rum. Spread this mixture on top of the layer of apricot jam. Use a pastry brush to brush the border on the puff pastry with water. Place the second piece of puff pastry on top, pressing the edges together to seal in the filling. Use a wooden skewer or toothpick to draw a zigzag pattern on top and then brush with the remaining whisked egg.
- Place the filled puff pastry in the preheated oven and bake for about 30 minutes or until the top appears golden brown in color and crisp to the touch. The galette can be served either warm or cold.

15

Parc Bonheur understood the meaning of hard work. Growing up he worked two to three jobs, several before the legal age, working a deal out with store managers who felt bad for the black kid – poor and, despite the common held belief that equality was rampant in France and the rest of the modern world, discriminated against. Parc's dad left when he was four, leaving behind his recovering drug-addict mom and three sisters. Being the oldest of his siblings and the only male in the house, Parc took it upon himself to make sure there was food on the table and that his mom had money to pay the bills, even if she only paid a small percentage of what was really due. But unlike many of his friends who were in similar situations, Parc had ambitions. He dreamt of some day buying his own flat in the heart of Paris, becoming a lawyer who could fight for little people, people like his mom and his friends, that needed someone to be their voice in a world where money bought power and power spent its time staring in a mirror, eventually drowning in self-obsession like Narcissus.

Parc did very little sleeping as a teenager, waking up early to shine shoes, going to classes, working as a stock boy at a local market, helping his occasionally unconscious mother prepare dinner for her kids, and then studying and finishing his homework before it all began the next day. Parc became an above average student, but, as one of his teachers in high school liked to point out to him on a regular basis, was not exceptional. Without help, there was no way he would get the scholarship he so desperately needed to afford to go to college and then to law school.

Thankfully his English teacher, Ms. Hardy, whose father just so happened to be a partner in the prestigious law firm, Hardy, Page & Palomer, took a liking to her hard-working student and wrote an impeccable letter of recommendation. With a bit of leaning from her father, Parc enrolled at Montpellier and then went on to the well-known Queen Mary, University of London in Paris, where he studied International Dispute Resolution and Economic Law.

All of the above precisely mentioned to acknowledge Parc's incredible intellect, which is why, today, running errands for a Mr. Palomer of Hardy, Page & Palomer, Parc was a little frustrated. He had been at the firm for nearly two years now and yet he was still just an errand-boy despite the title of "associate". Today, as the rest of the law firm met to discuss a prominent case regarding the country's largest steel manufacturer, Parc was out of the office and on his way to some bakery to pick up snacks for the other lawyers who had already ordered their blackcurrant macarons in anticipation of their mid-morning hunger that had apparently already struck an angry and ungrateful Mr. Palomer.

Parc pulled up to a little bakery tucked away in the shadow of the Eiffel Tower. "The Two Macarons," said Parc, reading the purple curly text on the sign above the door. "That's probably all a place this size can make," he thought. "Two macarons." Walking in, he wasn't surprised to find the place empty having noted the giant Delroy Doux across the street. Everyone in Paris, including the majority of his co-workers, raved about Double D, as they called it, their only complaint that the women working inside didn't always wear the matching bra size. Mr. Palomer, however, was from the old school of thought, ordering from The Two Macarons *because* they were more expensive – the more something costs the better it is. And, when you are rich, that way of thinking was easy, and fun, to live by. At least, Parc thought, he wouldn't have to wait in line like you do at Double D. He would be in and out in no time, back sooner than Mr. Palomer expected, which would not only make a good impression but might also give Parc a chance to listen in on the meeting, and, he thought, maybe even get a chance to say something.

Parc located a small copper bell on the middle counter top and tapped it, hoping to alert whoever was working of his presence. Parc counted to ten and checked his watch. His finger tapped the bell twice rapidly, hoping to send the signal that he was also in a hurry. He counted to ten again and let out a breath of exasperation. Three taps on the bell. His foot began to tap. Four taps on the bell. He began to look around anxiously, monitoring the kitchen door and then the front door for a sign of life. Nothing. I have to do something, Parc thought, and made his way through the kitchen door.

Immediately he saw his purple boxes, all labeled HP&P. Seeing as they had already been paid for in full, he planned on taking the boxes and rushing back to the office as quickly as possible, the idea of getting back sooner than he planned becoming more exciting as his imagination began going through the possible outcomes of his arrival. "Why Parc!" Mr. Palomer would exclaim. "Well done! What dedication! What motivation! What skill! Associate? No. Welcome back, partner."

But a mound of rich black hair bobbing up and down at the back of the bakery interrupted his plans. Out of the corner of his eye, Parc had spotted something, someone that made him stop dead in his tracks. Unconsciously he set down the boxes he was cradling in his arms, enthralled. He breathed deeply and closed his eyes, hoping to catch a scent of the goddess before him. Intoxicated by her sweet scent, like a fragrant rose fresh with morning dew, he opened his eyes and began to study her profile more closely. Her skin was perfect, soft, and pale with a peachy complexion in her cheeks. Her lips were full, plumped and pouty, painted with a rich red hue. Her dark hair looked rich and thick even though it was piled high on her head, casually thrown up to keep it out of her face.

She was absorbed in her work, her knife making strokes, an intricate pattern, in the puff pastry of her Galette Des Rois with the skill of a painter's paintbrush. She was listening to music, something she must love, classical, Parc guessed, smiling at the sound of each note, very much in a world of her own.

In moments like these the universe is kind, aware of schedules and repercussions, putting in use its great power to allow this moment to happen and freeze time. True love cannot be rushed. Hours go by in the lover's kitchen as a brief ten seconds tick by on the clock out front. The clock struck ten, the sound of the chime loud enough to crack time's ice block. Emerging from his reverie, Parc took a step towards his obsession and Tali slowly turned around to meet her fate.

CASSIS MACARONS

Serves 12

INGREDIENTS

- 2/3 cup ground almonds
- 1 ¾ cups powdered sugar
- ¼ cup finely ground sugar
- 3 large egg whites
- 2 teaspoons freeze dried blackcurrant powder (optional)
- 3-5 drops powdered food coloring
- For the filling
- ¾ cup chopped white chocolate or white chocolate chips
- ¼ cup cream
- 5 teaspoons cassis (blackcurrant) liqueur

DIRECTIONS

- Preheat your oven to 300 degrees F. Prepare two baking sheets by lining with parchment paper and set aside.
- In a mixing bowl whisk the egg whites until they form stiff peaks. Working in small batches, whisk in the finely ground sugar, alternating between the two. Then whisk in the blackcurrant powder (if using) and the food coloring until you achieve your desired color.
- Use a spatula to fold in the almonds and the powdered sugar until you create a thick but still batter-like consistency (pancake batter is too thin, cookie dough consistency is too thick). Place the dough in a pastry bag with a round tip and pipe onto the prepared baking trays leaving space between to allow for spreading. Let the macarons sit at room temperature for 15 minutes before placing in the preheated oven and baking for 12 minutes.
- Place pieces of parchment paper on top of your wire cooling racks and then transfer the baked cookies to cool completely.
- While the cookies cool prepare the filling by placing the cream and cassis liqueur in a saucepan over medium heat. Once just starting to bubble, begin to add in the white chocolate, mixing constantly until it melts completely and the mixture appears smooth.
- Spread the filling on the flat side of half of the macaron shells. Then place the remaining half of macarons on top, flat side down, pressing gently so that the filling just begins to poke out from the edges.

16

It is hard to find words to describe exactly what happens when two people fall in love at first sight, but if one could they would describe exactly what happened between Parc and Tali. In an instant they knew they would be together forever, but worldly conventions would make them wait before sealing the deal. For some reason, even in the most romantic city on earth, people didn't quite like the idea of two people getting married very quickly. There was something about the whole thing that made others insecure, as if they were personally jilted by the couple that had decided there was no one else on the planet (or at least within a hundred kilometer radius) that was better than the person they found and had fallen head over heels in love with.

Tali carried one of the three boxes outside to Parc's car, which had been running since he came in. His little red Peugeot reminded Tali of the small birds she listened to on warm days outside her window. Everything, Tali realized, about Parc reminded her of something she loved. She knew that she was already in love with Parc, but quickly turned her attention away from the idea, knowing that Margot and Zenna would give her a hard time for falling in love with a man she had just met and literally knew nothing about, except that he worked for a law firm that appreciated small businesses.

Parc took the third box out of Tali's arms, lingering for a moment, but moving away quickly aware as well that it was strange to have such strong emotions for a complete stranger. Saying goodbye and driving away was the hardest thing Parc had ever done. It took every ounce of willpower he had to not turn his car around, pick Tali up, and make love to her in the backseat. He didn't ask for her phone number or make plans to see her again, Parc realized as he turned the corner. The moment was too perfect, he thought, to ruin it with something as typical as a pick-up line. Besides, Parc didn't know what he would do with a girlfriend anyway. Trying to make his way through the law firm initiation consumed all of his time and energy. He had come so far now, he was so close - he couldn't give up. Parc hit the steering wheel with both hands in frustration, quickly correcting his ten and two position to avoid hitting a break dancing teenager who had strayed into the street.

Tali watched as Parc's car drove away, getting swallowed by the morning's traffic. The momentary disappointment she felt was quickly replaced with clarity. This is what true love was, she thought. This is what her parents had felt when they had first met. This was her "love at first sight" story and she knew that even though Parc left, giving her no idea when she would see him again, that their paths would cross again – and again and again until they became one. She had never been surer of anything in her life.

Turning to head back inside the empty bakery, she saw Zenna's unmistakable red hair strolling towards her. Her face was content and her hand was preoccupied, holding on to someone else's five fingers. The man whom the fingers belonged to, Tali decided, was adorable. He had a smile that was contagious, even from several meters away, and Tali suddenly caught herself smiling from ear to ear.

As the couple approached Tali racked her brain – who could this mystery man be? Should she know him? Ever since Tali had known Zenna she had never met any of the men in her life, primarily because they were rarely in her life for more than a night anyway.

"Good morning," Zenna chimed, her fingers still interlaced in those of her dashing escort. Tali greeted the two, unsure if she should introduce herself or wait for her friend to. But with a quick look at Zenna Tali realized to let the moment be theirs. She smiled and walked into the bakery, anxiously waiting to hear all about it. Too curious to leave the front of the bakery entirely, Tali made herself look busy, grabbing a cloth nearby and rubbing it in circular motions on the tables and backs of the chairs. She had a great view of the two from the front window, holding hands, staring into each other's eyes, laughing playfully and leaning into each other. Oh. My. Having just experienced what love looked like firsthand just moments ago, Tali knew in an instant. Her Zenna was madly in it.

Zenna came inside after watching her lover pull a unicycle out of a trunk of a car parked out front. He hopped on the one wheel, tipped his brown derby hat, and faded away into the shadows of soon to be bare trees. "That is Jacques," Zenna said, her smile so deliciously genuine Tali couldn't help but to squeal. "So..." Tali began, hoping to coax more details out of her friend. "So," Zenna replied, "I'm starved. I must have burnt a million calories last night." Zenna laughed, lingering by the front window, scanning the horizon to see if she could spot Jacques's house.

"Well then," Tali said, "It sounds like you could use some crepes." Tali headed back to the kitchen, wondering when both her and Zenna would see their men again. She had a feeling it would be very soon.

CREPES SUZETTE WITH ORANGE BUTTER

Serves 6

INGREDIENTS

- 2 large brown eggs
- ¾ cup all-purpose flour
- ½ cup milk
- 1/8 teaspoon sea salt
- ¼ teaspoon granulated sugar
- 1/3 cup ice cold water
- 1 tablespoon vegetable oil
- 1 tablespoon unsalted butter, melted
- For the butter
- 6 tablespoons unsalted butter, softened
- ¼ cup + 3 tablespoons granulated sugar
- 3 teaspoons freshly grated orange zest
- 1/3 cup fresh orange juice
- 1 ½ tablespoons cognac
- ¼ cup Grand Marnier

DIRECTIONS

- In a mixing bowl combine the eggs, flour, milk, salt, and sugar, whisking until smooth and thick. Add the water, oil, and melted butter, whisking again to combine.
- Rub a bit of butter into the bottom of a small nonstick skillet (about 6" or a crepe pan if available). Heat the skillet over medium-high heat. Place 2 tablespoons of the crepe batter into the prepared skillet, turning until it is distributed evenly on the bottom. After a minute, the edges of the crepe should begin to peel away from the sides. When this happens, flip the crepe. Cook the crepe on the other side for another 10 to 15 seconds or until the bottom starts to show a few brown spots. Turn the skillet over, tapping the crepe out onto a baking sheet. Continue preparing the crepes until all of the batter is used (you should be able to make a dozen crepes).
- To prepare the orange butter, combine the butter, ¼ cup sugar, and orange zest in a blender and run. Begin to add the orange juice a bit at a time with the blender still running until it all has been incorporated.
- Turn on your oven's broiler. Prepare a large baking sheet with a rim by rubbing the bottom with butter and then sprinkling with sugar. Place a crepe on the baking sheet

CREPES SUZETTE WITH ORANGE BUTTER 69

and then set 2 tablespoons of the orange butter in the center of it. Fold the crepe in half, sealing in the orange butter, and then fold it in half again to make a triangle shape. Continue with the remaining crepes until all are filled and folded. Arrange the crepes so that they all point the same direction, overlapping each other a bit. The remaining 3 tablespoons of sugar should be sprinkled over the finished crepes before placing in the broiler.

- Allow the sugar on the crepes to caramelize in the broiler, which should take about 2 minutes. Carefully transfer the crepes to a heatproof serving platter. In a small saucepan, combine the Grand Marnier and the cognac and heat over medium-high heat. Use a long match to light the alcohols on fire. While still flaming, pour over the crepes. Use a spoon to collect the alcohol that collects around the edges of the platter and continue pouring over the crepes until there are no more flames. Enjoy the crepes immediately.

17

Margot looked at her bakery beneath through the steel latticework of the Eiffel Tower. From her view, it looked as if The Two Macarons was closed, barred up, and very much out of business. It's only a matter of time before that perspective became reality, she thought. The way things were going her bakery would be closed by the end of January. She was late on her bills, she knew, could barely afford to buy the ingredients to make the desserts that no one bought, and, truth be told she was in a way relieved to be able to wash her hands of the whole mess.

She had become a walking disaster in recent months, floating through life like a dried-up leaf, just avoiding the inevitable – getting crushed. But now, looking at her empty bakery she decided it paired nicely with her empty life, which was only made bearable by night after night of meaningless sex. She was ready to be crushed, to leave this part of her life behind and move on, away from the stupid idea of a bakery, which she really had no idea how to run, and away from Paris. The fact that she had experienced success at all was pure luck. Or, maybe, she thought, life's cruel way of giving you something, like Aubin, only to pull it away by a string that was attached all along, maybe to teach you a lesson or maybe just to be a bitch.

Margot sat down on a bench, stalling going into the bakery for as long as she could today. If the bakery did close, what would she do with her life? Would she actually have the balls to move away? Maybe she would. Maybe she would jump on the train and head north, somewhere like Stockholm or Helsinki, where people were less romantic and more realistic, down-to-earth and driven, maybe there she could find herself, or at least be far enough away from the City Of Lights that she wouldn't have to be reminded of the romance, the life that could have been.

Laughing, Margot thought of another option - moving to the United States. There she could learn yoga, use her flexibility and alluring accent to steal men away from their girlfriends, and then fuck them just for the hell of it. She might not have luck on her side, but she was sure that karma hadn't deserted her. And karma definitely owed her one.

She stood up, deciding that she would figure out an exit plan soon enough. Only a few more weeks in Paris, a few more weeks as owner of The Two Macarons, and then she would disappear. She liked that idea. But then, as she approached the sidewalk in front of her bakery, she caught a glimpse of Zenna, happily arranging the pastries in the front, smiling and chatting with Basile. She thought about Zenna's son and how sweet he was. She thought about having to tell Zenna she was out of a job. Telling Coty that his mom no longer had money to pay rent for the apartment he had come to know as home.

And then there was Basile. The bakery was his home and meant more to him than she could understand. Basile needed the bakery just like Zenna, just like Coty.

Her heart sank. She couldn't just let all of this crumble. Margot had been called lots of names in her life, slut, bitch, blonde, but never conceited, and she meant to keep it that way.

"Damn it," Margot sighed, knowing that she would have to fight and fight hard to keep the bakery open. Even if she didn't want it anymore, she knew three people who desperately needed it. And she was not going to be the one to take it away from them.

An old woman and her two grandchildren approached the door of the bakery just as Margot was about to go inside herself. "Allow me," Margot said as she opened the door, hoping to make a good impression, for what would most likely their only customer that afternoon. The woman, who was dressed in blue riding pants, brown knee-high boots, and a wool sweater, white like her hair, took her grandchildren, a little boy about five and a girl maybe six or seven still in their uniforms having just got out of school, by the hand up to peek inside the cases, asking them to say the colors and names of each dessert.

"Let me know how I can help you," Margot said to her, making her way behind the counter and slipping on her apron, whispering an apology for her tardiness to Zenna.

"It will take us a bit to get through all of these," the woman said, looking up at Zenna and Margot with a smile.

"No hurry," Margot replied, leaving her in the hands of Zenna as she made her way to the back to see what Tali was up to.

Tali appeared uncharacteristically happy, almost chipper. There was a glow about her Margot observed, as if she had swallowed something radioactive. Or, more likely, Margot decided considering Tali's graceful and unhurried movements, like she were shot by a very large arrow by a notorious naked angel. In fact, the arrow was still protruding right out of her back, directly behind her heart. Margot prepared herself for a conversation with love-drugged Tali, trying to muster up the best attitude possible so as not to offend her. Margot was actually a bit intrigued – who could have won Tali's heart? She was always so reserved and quiet. Had she even spoke with the guy? Maybe it was just a crush.

Having noticed Margot's presence and unable to hold her enamored tongue any longer Tali wiped the flour off her hands onto her white apron and looked Margot in the eyes, grinning like a little girl who just blew out all the candles on her birthday cake. "I met someone," she said nearly in a whisper, not wanting to scare the love away.

"I can tell," Margot laughed.

Tali in love, Margot thought. That's interesting. Actually, everything about Tali was interesting. She was unquestionably the most beautiful woman Margot had ever seen in person and yet she emitted some sort of "Don't-Fuck-With-Me" vibe that kept the majority of men at bay. Tali was quiet, reserved, and even when faced with the advances of incredibly attractive men, managed to turn them away, cool but kind, her face serious enough to make sure they would never try again. In Margot's mind, there was a very good chance Tali had never been laid in her life, which was such a pity, an incredible waste.

Margot knew many men who would pay top dollar for a girl like that. So much money, in fact, that after a couple nights she could save her bakery (and probably buy herself a nice pair of shoes while she was at it!) Prostitute Tali. Margot played with the idea as she broke Tali's just made Nougat Noir with the back of her knife. The slab broke into small pieces, getting her hands dirty, dirty like Tali could, and would, become. Margot The Pimptress – it had a nice ring to it. Tali even had a room practically upstairs. The bakery could become a front for a very lucrative business. She had all the ingredients, now she just had to convince Tali to hop in the oven.

She looked at Tali with the eyes of a potential nighttime client. She would definitely do – do well, do hard, do long, and orgasm with mouth open, hands gripping the headboard behind her.

Tali, aware of Margot's penetrating stare, guessed that she wanted to hear more about the man she was in love with so she added, "He's handsome." She blushed as she smiled. Hmm, Margot thought smiling back at Tali, it would be harder than she thought to get Tali on board with her new idea, realizing that not everyone was as sexually enlightened as she was.

Margot began to prepare another batch of the dark nougat, the almost black color matching her perverse plan. As she mixed the sugar and honey together over the stainless steel stove, she wondered exactly how much a doe-eyed virgin like Tali would go for in today's sex market.

NOUGAT NOIR

Serves 6 to 12

(The more sinister the plot the more you will need to eat)

INGREDIENTS

- 1 pound roasted almonds, hot
- 1/3 pound roasted hazelnuts, hot
- 8 ½ tablespoons honey
- 1 1/3 cup granulated sugar

DIRECTIONS

- Prepare a large marble slab by greasing with oil or butter. If you want to use a silicone baking sheet instead you won't need to grease it.
- Combine the sugar and honey together in a saucepan and heat over medium. Use a candy thermometer to monitor the mixture until it reaches 330 degrees F. Then stir in the roasted nuts and mix thoroughly. Pour the hot candy mixture onto the greased slab or silicone sheet, using the back of a spoon to spread it evenly.
- Allow the mixture to cool and harden for 10 minutes. Then use a knife to cut the nougat into small, bite size pieces. Allow the candy to cool for another 10 minutes before serving or packaging in airtight containers.

18

Zenna was enjoying watching the woman and her two grandchildren delight in the displays of pastry in the front cases, darting back and forth, commenting on the decoration. Seeing people's eyes light up in response to what she had made was her favorite part about baking. Unfortunately, people weren't always aware of the pleasure bakers get from having their work admired, especially when in a hurry, saying nothing more than a "that there" and "thanks" before leaving. That's why children were Zenna's favorite. They were never in a rush and spoke their minds, giving her sound feedback and ideas for her next confections.

Spotting Coty walking through the front door, still in his school uniform too, backpack slung over one shoulder, Zenna excused herself from behind the counter for a moment to ask her son how his last day was before Christmas break and if he was hungry, which of course he was. Coty took a seat at the table behind Basile, pulling out pages of arithmetic that were due in January when he returned to school.

Zenna shook her head. What kind of teacher would assign a 5-year-old homework, especially over a long vacation? Hoping to cheer him up she brought Coty a cup of warm chocolate. She kneeled on the ground next to Coty's chair, looking over his shoulder to double-check his work, $1+1 = 2$, $2+2 = 4$, and so on. "You're doing great, sweetie," Zenna said hugging Coty as she rocked forward to stand up and get Coty the special snack she had made him earlier this afternoon.

But the intense look on Basile's face stopped Zenna from getting up. Basile was turned slightly in his chair, enough that she could see his profile from her position behind him.

Having shifted his gaze away from the book, Basile was focused on the face of the old woman at the counter. This type of behavior was extremely unusual for Basile. He was not the type to come to a public spot to people watch. To the contrary Basile came to places like the bakery to escape the real world, often so caught up in his book or work that he very rarely even looked up to check the time or observe whatever commotion might be occurring in the bakery. He was there solely for his coffee, his pastry, and his three "French Hens" – nothing more.

Zenna remembered the time last summer that an entire busload of nude tourists unloaded in front of the bakery. Loud and exuberant, the group began shouting about taking pictures of The Tower. The nudists laughed, picked their cameras up off their bare chests, and began pointing their lenses not in the direction of The Tower Zenna assumed they had meant (The Eiffel, of course, like every other busload that comes through every hour), but rather at a man who had began posing on a bench just outside the bakery's window, legs wide to flank the enormous erection he had on display. After getting their picture of *the tower*, many of the tourists began coming inside the bakery, placing orders, waving penises, breasts, and vaginas in every direction. And dear old Basile didn't even look up once.

Today, however, was very different. Basile's focus was glued on this lovely old woman who was now standing at the counter ready to place an order for herself and her two little companions. Realizing that she needed to move but not wanting to break the spell that Basile was under, Zenna quietly stood up and walked the back way behind the counter. Basile remained so stoic that Zenna thought for a brief moment that he may have had a stroke.

"Just a moment," said the woman, acknowledging the tug on her pocket that came from a little boy who had changed his mind about what he wanted. While Zenna waited for minds to be made up, she pulled out the apple tart she had made for Coty and sprinkled the top with gold leaf flecks to add a bit of Christmas magic for her son who was still working away on his homework.

The woman stood up, having just had the final decision whispered into her ear, as Zenna simultaneously ran her hand over the counter, brushing the stray gold flecks into the air. The small puff of gold floated just above the woman's head, catching the sunlight just right so that they illuminated her face with a brilliant glow as they floated down to the floor. The woman glowed for only a brief moment, a moment so brief, in fact, that unless someone was looking for it, it would have been missed entirely.

"You have a lovely bakery," the woman smiled at Zenna. "It was so hard to make up our minds!" She reached her hand forward. "I'm Oralie. I don't think we have met." Zenna shook her hand and introduced herself, pleased to put their order in a small box to take home (three macarons – all different colors, a pink napoleon decorated with snowflakes, a cream puff drizzled with chocolate, and a small pumpkin pie that Oralie said was for a get-together she was having tonight with a few friends.)

Oralie handed the box to the little boy, who was happy to be entrusted with such an important duty, and took the hand of the little girl. As they made their way out of the bakery Oralie paused and smiled at Basile, who was still entranced and unable to acknowledge her, let alone her beautiful gesture.

Coty, who had taken a break from his boring math work, watched this scene from his seat at the table behind Basile. Despite his young age, Coty understood every look, every gesture. Although they rarely talked, Basile was near and dear to Coty's heart. Growing up without a father was hard on Coty and he desperately wanted a male figure in his life. Age didn't matter, Coty thought. As long as the man was respectful and kind and, most importantly, present, he would do just fine as a dad. Basile, in Coty's eyes, was the closest thing he had to a real dad and, seeing now that his dad was in love, he made a pact with himself to make sure that the old woman who had just left would fall in love with Basile too and, like his mom would read to him from his bedtime stories, would "live happily ever after and have a lot of children." Coty needed a good idea, one that would bring the two together forever.

Zenna returned to Coty's table with a just-cut slice of apple tart dusted with gold, much to Coty's amazement. He grabbed his fork and dug in, his mind busy with romantic plans. Zenna tousled his hair with her fingers and, seeing as there were no other customers in the bakery, took a seat on the other side of the table. She stole a bite of the tart and decided to help him finish his work so that he could enjoy his Christmas break. Stupid teachers, she thought, as she wrote 3+3 = 6.

FRENCH APPLE TART WITH GOLD DUST

Serves 8

INGREDIENTS

- 1 ¼ cups flour + 1 tablespoon
- 12 tablespoons unsalted butter, cubed into tablespoons, cold
- ¼ teaspoon kosher salt
- 3 tablespoons ice cold water
- 7 green baking apples, peeled, cored, and sliced in half
- ¼ cup granulated sugar
- ¾ cup apricot jam
- Gold leaf flakes, for dusting

DIRECTIONS

- Place the flour, 8 tablespoons of the butter, and salt into a large mixing bowl. Use a pastry blender to combine until the mixture is crumbly with pea-size chunks. Slowly add the water, using a spatula to mix in and moisten the dough.

- Flour a work surface and turn the dough out on it. Use your hands or a rolling pin to create a flat oval shape and cover in plastic wrap. Place it in the refrigerator for 1 hour. Remove the plastic wrap and place the dough back on a floured work surface. Use a rolling pin to create a 13" circle. Lay the dough in the bottom of an 11" tart pan that has a removable bottom. Use a small knife to remove the overhanging edges, cover with plastic wrap, and place the tart pan in the refrigerator for another hour.

- Set your oven's temperature to 375 degrees F. Prepare the apples by slicing into thin sections. Arrange the apple slices decoratively in the pan, starting from the outside and working in. Sprinkle the granulated sugar on top of the apples. Take the remaining 4 tablespoons of butter and dot the top of the tart. Set the pan in the preheated oven and bake for about 65 minutes or until the top and edges become golden brown. When the tart is done baking, set the pan on top of a cooling rack and cool completely.

- As the tart bakes, place the apricot jam in a small pan and warm over the stove until its consistency starts to thin. Pour the warm jam into a strainer over a small bowl. Once the tart has finished baking, brush the strained jam over the top of the tart.

- Just before serving, dust each slice with a generous sprinkle of edible gold leaf flakes.

19

"I think Basile is in love!" Zenna announced to her friends in the back. "Aw, that's so cute," grinned Tali, the fact that everyone, including herself, was finding love and at this special time of the year too, made her giddy. Zenna and Tali, being very much in love, a new feeling for both of them, were enjoying each other's company today more than usual. Margot, on the other hand, was feeling not only left out, but her bad attitude from the morning had come back with a vengeance. Everything around her was depressing, even the Tarte Tatin on the counter, baked, browned, and upside down seemed to mock her. Yes, her life was indeed upside down at the moment or, to use Margot's choice word, fucked.

Without consciously making the decision, Margot had given up on love ever since breaking up with Aubin. What else does a person do when what they honestly believed to be real turned out to be as fake as the boobs on the bimbo blonde Aubin left her for? Not looking for love but wanting to show her friends that she was fine, Margot went on a sex binge, sleeping with several different men every week. Which is exactly why she couldn't blame her friends now who were clearly rubbing their new romances in her face at this very moment. Her friends believed her when she said she was happy. They believed her when she said that she was glad to be out of the confinement of a relationship and into something that seemed much more natural, albeit primal. They listened to her stories about mind-blowing sex from the night before, laughed when she ignored the phone calls from men who wanted to see her again, and they nodded as she explained that women could want sex just like men want sex – for the experience, no strings attached.

But the truth was that Margot was miserable. She was falling apart inside even though outside she looked to be picture perfect, and in Prada. She hated how she felt leaving a man's apartment after meaninglessly screwing him. Even though she thought the experience would be liberating, putting her in control, it turned out that it made her feel used. She had the strange feeling that over the past several months her insides were starting to rot, what used to be healthy and bright corners of her body were crumbling into dust. She was desperate to find something to make her come alive again. Maybe it would be saving her bakery for her friends. Maybe it would be finding someone who really loved her, baggage and all.

Looking at Tali and Zenna who were busy at work, basking in their lovers' glow, Margot, feeling very much out of place, decided to find something to do in the front of the bakery. She busied her hands with cleaning and rearranging, all things which used to be important but now, looking at all of the empty chairs and the people walking by without so much as a glance through the window, clearly were not.

There must be something I can do, Margot thought. There must be something that will keep me from dying alone with twenty cats. She looked out the window and noticed that snow had begun to fall, just a few flakes, but still, she hoped, maybe a sign that things were about to change.

TARTE TATIN

Serves 10

INGREDIENTS

- 1 2/3 cups all-purpose flour
- 1 large egg yolk, whisked
- ¾ teaspoon kosher salt
- 3 tablespoons water
- 6 tablespoons unsalted butter, softened
- For the filling
- 5 green baking apples, peeled, cored, and sliced in half
- 8 tablespoons (1/2 cup) unsalted butter
- 1 ½ cups granulated sugar

DIRECTIONS

- Prepare a clean work surface. Place the flour into a sifter and sift into a mound on the prepared surface. Use your fingers to make a well in the center. Drop the egg yolk, salt, water, and butter into the well. Use a hand to work the flour into the well, combining the ingredients until well mixed. When finished the dough should form with large soft crumbs. Use your hands to press the dough together to form a ball – it's okay if the dough ball doesn't look perfect in consistency, as it will be blended more in a moment.

- Flour your work surface and then place the dough ball on top. Use the heel of your hand to knead the dough for 1 to 2 minutes or until it becomes pliable and stays in one piece. Form a ball and cover with plastic wrap. Place the dough in the refrigerator for about 20 minutes or until it is firm.

- As the dough chills, place the butter for the filling in a 10" nonstick, ovenproof skillet. Heat the butter over medium heat, adding the sugar and cooking (don't stir yet) until the mixture caramelizes and becomes brown. Using a wooden spoon, gently stir the mixture until it forms a deep brown caramel. This should take about 8 minutes total from start to finish. Remove the skillet from the heat and allow the caramel to cool for 5 minutes.

- Arrange the apples close together on top of the caramel in the skillet, working in concentric circles starting from the edges of the pan. Return the skillet to medium heat and cook the apples for 6 to 8 minutes or until their juices begin to run. Bump the heat up to high and continue cooking the apples until the bottoms caramelize and the juice has evaporated, about 20 minutes. If necessary, reduce the heat slightly as the apples cook to prevent the caramel from bubbling over the sides.

- Use a fork to turn the apples over and continue cooking so the second side has a chance to caramelize, about another 15 minutes. When finished the apples should look golden with very little juice if any remaining. Take the skillet off the heat and allow them to cool in the pan.

- Set your oven's temperature to 400 degrees F.

- Remove the dough from the refrigerator and place on a floured work surface. Use a rolling pin to roll the dough so that it is just larger than the skillet in which the apples were cooked. Use the rolling pin to transfer the dough on top of the cooling apples, tucking the edges quickly around the sides. Use a wooden skewer to poke a hole in the top of the dough so that steam can get out.

- Place the skillet in the preheated oven and bake for about 25 minutes or until the dough has become firm and slightly browned on top. Once finished baking, allow the tart to cool for 10 minutes. You want the tart to still be warm before turning upside down, so if you're not eating it right away keep it in the pan and then re-heat in the oven for a few minutes to soften the caramel and free the apples.

- Place a rimmed serving plate on top of the skillet, carefully flipping over to free the tart from the pan. Use caution when doing this as hot juice can burn you. Use a knife to slice the finished tart into wedges and enjoy warm.

20

The girls were so busy watching for people not to come into their bakery that they missed someone who did. A Mr. Jules Lorance happened by the bakery earlier that afternoon not looking for food, he couldn't eat when he worked, but for a place with a table, preferably one very quiet, where he could put pen to paper. Looking in through the large front window, he figured the bakery must be closed for some sort of renovation, considering the lack of people inside. He tried the door anyway and to his surprise it opened with ease. It was warm inside the bakery. The smell was incredible. And the silence that he was met with was undeniably perfect. Seeing as no one was in the front at that moment, Jules decided to sit down and get to work. If anyone approached him to say that the table was for customers only, he would order a cup of coffee and get back to work. Ideas began to flow better than they had in weeks for Mr. Lorance, leaving him so absorbed in his work that he became invisible, both to himself and the Three French Hens.

Unbeknownst to Mr. Lorance, his inspiration was flowing from the mind of the blonde woman who was busying herself on the other side of the bakery behind the counter. The silence of the bakery had become so intense that Margot's personal thoughts were audible to her and the only other person listening, Jules. The thought waves traveled through Jules's left ear and into the pen in his right hand, filling page after page with literary gold. Over the next several hours Jules learned more about Margot than most people learn about each other in years, her deepest fears, her most secret insecurities, her fantasies, and her dreams for the future.

Looking up from his pages of work, Jules noticed that the sun had already set, amused that he had been working at this little bakery for so long. He wondered why no one had approached him to ask him what he was doing or to say that the shop was closing? Maybe he had been locked in, but a few of the lights in the front were still on, which must mean that someone was still here. Considering that he still had light to write and the fact that he was writing so well, he decided to stay until he was asked to leave.

Meanwhile, Margot, who was still lost in her thoughts on the other side of the bakery, decided to take a break from the meaningless work she had been occupied with and take a seat. She collapsed into a wooden chair, more exhausted mentally than physically. Margot, without warning, began to cry, worn out from the past several months. She had hit her breaking point and couldn't even attempt to contain the tears that were now rushing down her face.

The sound of Margot's crying reached the ears of Jules, who quietly turned around to search for the source. A few tables back he spotted a mess of curly blonde hair crumpled on top of the table. In an instant he understood. This, he realized, is the woman he had been writing about all afternoon. This was Margot. Not sure what his next move should be, he decided to try to quietly sneak by her, not wanting to embarrass her by his presence. He gathered up his papers and successfully moved his chair away from the table without making a sound. His black loafers began to tiptoe across the wood floor, but as he neared Margot's table his clumsy foot caught the edge of another chair, creating a loud scratching noise, which immediately alerted Margot to his presence.

Margot's pile of hair shot up off the surface of the table, her hand instantly moving to her face to try to hide the evidence of her emotional breakdown. "I'm so sorry," said Jules, admitting failure to his spoiled escape.

"I didn't know anyone was here," Margot said, admiring the handsome face of the man before her.

He wasn't obviously her type. He was a bit older than she was and his hair, although thick, was slightly graying. He was of average height, which to Margot meant he was short. He was dressed casually in jeans and a crimson sweater, a collar of a button-up shirt sticking out of the top. But there was something about him that made it impossible for Margot to look away. He looked kind and his dark brown eyes stared at her as if they knew everything about her.

Curious to meet the woman that he had gotten to know so well, Jules took a seat at Margot's table. "Margot, right?" he said in an English accent. She nodded, wondering how he knew her. "I know things seem real shitty right now, but I know for a fact that they are going to get better," he continued. The confidence of this stranger made Margot laugh.

"Who are you?" she asked.

"Jules. Jules Lorance. I'm a writer. Your bakery, you actually, have inspired me all afternoon. I have never written so much so well in a few hours."

Margot blushed at his complement, but then realized that he had said *hours*. Had he been here all afternoon? Had he been staring at her while she worked?

"Quite to the contrary," Jules explained. "I had no inkling that anyone was here but me." He looked Margot intensely in the eyes. "I walked in, sat down, and was suddenly inspired to write about a beautiful woman, a woman who has given up on love," he paused, searching Margot's face for permission to continue. Finding it he continued,

"A woman who is torn between running away from her past or sacrificing her happiness for that of her friends. She is proud and confident, but deep down she is afraid."

"Afraid of what?" asked Margot, curious to see if this stranger could help her sort out her screwed up life.

"She is afraid to be honest. Terrified at the idea that people might see her for what she really is – someone who desperately wants to fall in love, someone who wants to be taken care of." Jules suddenly remembered that he wasn't just talking about a character in his book, but a real person who was sitting directly in front of him. Jules realized he might be saying too much, so he stopped.

"Are you hungry?" she asked. "I'm starved," she said as she got up from the table. "Do you like cream puffs, Jules?"

But Jules was unable to answer, too busy staring at the perfect body in front him. Margot's tight dress accentuated her curves and her silver flecked stockings hugged her thin, but muscular legs, which were worked everyday from the heels she walked miles in.

Margot returned with a box of cream puffs from the back. "Someone ordered these but never picked them up," she said as she bit into a fluffy pastry. Margot proceeded to lick the cream that had oozed out of the puff off her fingers, tantalizing poor Jules who looked helplessly at the sexual goddess before him. He had never been so turned on by a woman and knowing Margot's past, he guessed that if he came onto her there was a good possibility that they would be having sex somewhere in the bakery within the next thirty minutes.

But as much as Jules wanted Margot right then and there, he couldn't bring himself to take advantage of her. A one-night stand wasn't his style and Margot deserved more. She deserved someone that respected her and that wanted her more than just for hot sex. In his story, he decided, Margot's perfect type would be someone that was intellectual. Someone with enough money to take care of her, but not so much that she would be attracted to him just for that and that alone. She needed to be with someone older than herself, someone that appreciated her beauty, her youth, and her confidence without feeling intimidated.

As he thought about who is character should end up with at the end, he discovered that the person he was describing sounded startlingly like him. Yes, Margot needed to be with a British writer. Margot needed to end up with Jules.

"So," said Margot breaking the silence after finishing her second cream puff. "How does this woman find that? Tell me what happens next."

Recognizing that this was his opportunity to make a play for the woman of his dreams Jules said, "Well, really it's up to her. There are lots of ways I can finish the story, I just need to get to know her better so I know what she wants."

"What if," Margot started running her fingers through her hair, "this woman was crazy, like a murderer? What would happen next?"

Laughing at her playfulness Jules said,

"In that case she would lure a nice foreign man into her apartment, asking him to fix her heater. He would gladly help her, seeing how stunning she was, and then she would strangle him with the cord from the drapes in her living room. She would continue her strangling rampage all across Europe until a dashing detective caught her. Being so charming, the detective would fall in love with her and ruin the case against her. They would get married but on their honeymoon night he would see her emerging from the bathroom with a hair dryer, playing villainously with the cord. She would get into bed with him and that's where the story would end."

"So no one would know if she killed him or used the cord to tie him up for sex?" asked Margot.

"Right," said Jules smiling, briefly imagining what it would be like to be tied up by a naughty vixen like her.

"Okay, so what if instead of being a murder-mystery your story was erotic? What would happen to the woman next?" Margot asked, anxious to hear what Jules would say.

"That," said Jules, biting his lip, "would result in a lot of sex scenes, which would mean I would really need to get familiar with sex with this woman myself so that I could, of course, accurately portray her encounters through my writing." Jules laughed out of nervousness, unable to believe that he really just said that aloud.

Thankfully, Margot took it well and smiled saying, "That's fair." Margot was really beginning to like this Jules guy.

"Alright, last scenario. What if the woman in your story wanted her story to end like a fairy tale? What if she was secretly a princess? What would happen then?"

"Ah ha," he said, glad that she brought this version of the story up because he knew that this is exactly what she wanted.

"Well in that case," he began, "she would be in her store late one night. She would think she was alone but really a prince had snuck in, desperately hoping to sweep her off her feet. They would get into an interesting conversation, filled with sexual innuendos and lots of pastry. The prince would be so charming that the woman would instantly fall in love."

"Oh really?" said Margot raising her eyebrow. "And then what would happen? A horse-drawn carriage would pull up in the snow out front, ready to carry me away from all of this and back to your castle in the hills?"

"You tell me," Jules said, gesturing out the window to the horse-drawn sleigh that had just pulled up out front. Margot froze, unable to believe her eyes. Was this really happening? She pinched her leg under the table just to be sure.

"So, does she choose the fairy tale?" Jules asked standing up and offering her his hand. Margot slowly got up from the table and put her hand in his. How could she not?

CREAM PUFFS

Serves 16

INGREDIENTS

- ½ cup whole milk
- 8 tablespoons unsalted butter, divided into tablespoon-size pieces
- 1 teaspoon + 2 tablespoons granulated sugar
- 1 teaspoon kosher salt
- ½ cup water
- 1 cup all-purpose flour
- 6 large brown eggs
- 2 ¼ cups heavy cream
- Powdered sugar, for topping

DIRECTIONS

- Prepare 2 baking sheets by lining with parchment paper and a large pastry bag with a regular ½" fitted tip. Preheat your oven to 450 degrees F.

- In a medium size saucepan combine the milk, butter, a teaspoon of sugar, salt, and water. Bring everything to a boil over medium-heat, stirring occasionally. Add the flour and lower the heat to medium-low. Continue stirring until the mixture forms a dough that pulls away from the sides. This should take a couple of minutes. Stir for another minute until a thin film is created on the bottom of the pan. Then transfer the mixture to a bowl.

- Place 1 egg in the bowl with the dough mixture and stir until the egg is completely mixed in, which should take about 2 minutes. Continue the same process with 4 more eggs, working 1 egg at a time. Once the 5 eggs are added, the dough should look smooth and thick.

- Transfer the dough into the prepared pastry bag and pipe onto the prepared baking sheets in 2 ½" circles. Leave about 2" between each circle.

- In a small bowl combine the remaining egg with a couple teaspoons of water, whisking until smooth. Use a pastry brush to brush the tops of the dough rounds and then place in the preheated oven. As soon as the sheets go in, turn OFF the oven and set the timer for 10 minutes. After 10 minutes, turn the oven back ON at 350 degrees F. When finished baking, the puffs should be deep golden in color. Place the baked puffs on a cooling rack and cool completely.

- Once cool, use a sharp knife to slice off the top quarter of each puff. Place the removed tops on a plate and use your finger to press down the center of each puff, which should still be a bit doughy.

- Place a ½" fancy tip on a clean pastry bag. In a large bowl, combine the heavy cream and remaining 2 tablespoons of sugar. Beat the mixture until it holds soft peaks. Transfer the whipped cream into the prepared pastry bag and fill the bottom portion of each puff with a generous amount. Sprinkle the tops of the puffs with granulated sugar and place on top of the cream-filled halves.

21

December 24th - It's amazing how so much change can happen in one day. Love can be ignited, life can be created, death can come knocking, and hope can be restored. Another day had arrived at The Two Macarons, but Margot was nowhere to be found. Tali had opened the store that morning and ten minutes later Zenna arrived with Coty, who got to work writing a letter to Pere Noel telling him all about what he was up to today, how school was going, what the weather was like, and adding at the end, of course, what he would hope to receive tomorrow morning. Both women were having a great day, momentarily forgetting the looming possibility of the bakery closing. Love, they discovered, was more powerful than any other emotion, giving all who accept it the power of invincibility – nothing, they thought, could ruin their day.

At 9:26 in the morning a man in a suit walked into the bakery. "I represent Mr. Delroy Tasse and his new business partner, Aubin Guillory. They have just signed the papers to buy this building. Considering that the owner of…" he glanced down at the papers in his hand. "The owner of The Two Macarons is behind on her rent, I have been ordered to evict unless the rent for this month and all previous missed months is paid by Monday, December 26th."

The man looked at Tali and Zenna to make sure they understood the significance of what he had just said and, based on their angry expressions, they had.

"You know, Mr. Tasse is considerate. I said the payment should be due tomorrow, but he said to give an extra day in light of the Christmas holiday."

He set his stack of legal papers on the table for the girls to look over. "I'll be back Monday," he said as he walked out the door. "If you don't have the money, Mr. Tasse and Mr. Guillory have ordered that this little bakery closes immediately."

"Delroy and Aubin are buying the building?" said Zenna flustered. "Those fucking bastards." Tali, who just realized that this could also impact the art gallery that she worked in as well as her little home above it, was speechless. What would she do? If the bakery closed she wouldn't have a paycheck. If the art gallery closed she couldn't get another paycheck. The chances of another gallery in town agreeing to sell her work were slim. No paycheck meant no place to live. Tali would have to move back with her aunt in Swansea and leave her City of Lights, her memories of her parents, her dream of becoming an artist all behind.

"We need Margot," Tali said desperately, hoping that she would know what to do in light of the breaking news.

"She's not answering her phone," said Zenna setting her cell phone on the counter.

She was worried too. This was the most stable her life had ever been. She was doing what she loved and her son was thriving, no longer having to spend his afternoons performing on the streets or begging for food. But her parents were only helping her and Coty now because she had this job at the bakery. They said they were proud of her, but, they reminded her one evening over a glass of wine, would fight for custody of Coty if she lost her respectable job. The bakery closing could mean that she wouldn't get to raise her son, to wake up with him in the morning and listen to him tell her about his dreams over waffles, to kiss him goodnight and fall asleep holding his hand on the floor next to him. If the bakery closed, her life would be over.

"Is everything okay mommy?" asked Coty, looking up from his crayon-written letter and noticing his mom's worried face. "Yes," she said, lying. "Everything is just fine." Coty smiled at his mom and got back to work.

"Tali," Zenna said quietly. "I don't know what we can do, but I know that if I don't bake something right now I'm going to fucking lose my mind." Tali saw the tears forming in the corners of her friend's eyes. She realized that the bakery closing would affect everyone in the room, everyone she had come to love. "Okay," she said, trying to be upbeat. "Let's bake."

The two girls headed to the back, taking out the ingredients for a simple Gateau Basque. In moments like this, where everything suddenly seemed like it could come crashing down without notice, it was important to bake something simple. On Christmas Eve, no other bakery in Paris would be spending their time baking something so plain, so unusual, but the simplicity of this filled cake, one that Zenna learned to make from her grandmother that grew up in Southern France, began to calm the girls, allowing them to believe that maybe, just maybe, everything would be okay. Christmas miracles can happen, right?

GATEAU BASQUE

Serves 8

INGREDIENTS

- 2 cups all-purpose flour
- ¾ teaspoons baking powder
- ½ teaspoon kosher salt
- 10 tablespoons unsalted butter, at room temperature
- ¼ cup light brown sugar, packed
- ¼ cup granulated sugar
- 1 egg, at room temperature
- ½ teaspoon vanilla extract
- 3/4 cup jam (cherry, raspberry, strawberry, etc.)
- For the glaze
- 1 egg
- ¼ cup water

DIRECTIONS

- Combine the flour, baking powder, and salt in a mixing bowl; whisk to combine.

- In a larger mixing bowl, combine the butter, sugar, and brown sugar. Beat with an electric mixer for 3 minutes on medium speed or until smooth. Add the egg and continue beating for another 2 minutes. Mix in the vanilla. Adjust your mixer's speed to low and mix in the dry ingredients, working in small batches, until a sticky dough forms.

- Cover your work surface with wax paper and transfer half of the dough onto it. Place another piece of wax paper on top of the dough and use a rolling pin to flatten until it is 8" in diameter. Repeat with the other half of the dough. Set your 2 dough rounds on a baking sheet (still on the wax paper) and place in the refrigerator for at least 3 hours (or up to 2 days).

- Preheat your oven to 350 degrees F. Prepare an 8" round cake pan by greasing. Remove the wax paper from the chilled dough. Place one layer in the bottom of the prepared pan, pressing down and up the edges if necessary. Spoon the jam on top and spread into an even layer, leaving a small border of dough. Splash the exposed dough of the bottom layer with water and then place the top layer of the cake on top. Use your finger to press the edges together to seal the jam in.

- Combine the ingredients for the glaze in a small bowl and whisk. Use a pastry brush to coat the top of the cake with the glaze. Create a pattern in the top of the cake using the tines of the fork; a simple crosshatch design is traditional.

- Set the cake in the preheated oven and bake for about 40 minutes or until the top becomes golden brown. Allow the cake to cool in the pan on a wire rack for 5 to 10 minutes. Then take a blunt knife and run it around the edges of the cake to loosen it from the pan. Invert the cake onto a plate and then invert again onto the cooling rack so that it can cool right side up. Allow the cake to cool to room temperature before slicing and enjoying.

22

Minutes before the clock in the front of The Two Macarons struck noon, Margot and Jules walked in through the front door, bundled up, arms linked. Jules didn't look like the typical guy Margot had taken a liking to in the past few weeks, which relieved, and confused, Tali and Zenna. Jules kissed Margot on the lips and left, but took advantage of the large front window, taking one last look at the beautiful woman he spent last night with, unable to believe his good fortune.

"Who was that?" asked Zenna, hoping Margot would spill all of the beans, not leaving out one juicy detail.

"That," Margot answered, "is what is going to help us save this bakery."

"Did you hear we're going to be evicted by Delroy Tasse and Aubin?" said Tali, hoping that Margot was already aware of the latest threat to her business.

"No," she said, pausing to register what she just heard, "but it doesn't matter. We are going to destroy Delroy Doux tonight and tomorrow, when all of Paris is left without a place to go for their Christmas desserts, our bakery will be filled."

Zenna and Tali's hearts sank. The plan sounded too good to be true and very much lacking in necessary details. How were they going to make all the money they needed for rent, almost 3,200 Euros, in one day? But at least, Zenna thought, they were going to try.

"So how are we going to take out Delroy Doux?" they asked.

"We're going to Crème Brulee it," Margot replied with a smile, apparently not hearing how ridiculous her idea sounded.

"No really, what's the plan?" said Zenna, who was a little frustrated that Margot was making light of the seriousness of the situation. Maybe Margot didn't really want to save the bakery, she thought. Margot knew a lot of people in Paris, many in the elite class, who would gladly get her a job. Plus, she could nab a guy with money in a second and be taken care of for the rest of her life. The fact that Margot didn't need the bakery like she did scared the shit out of Zenna, who decided that she might need to take things into her own hands.

"I'm serious," said Margot, explaining that her plan wouldn't hurt anyone but would attract spectators, which meant lots of people in the area. When Delroy Doux would have to close to fix the damage done by the caramelized sugar coating, people would be forced to get their Christmas morning pastries at the next closest bakery, The Two Macarons.

"All we need is a ton of sugar, a giant torch, some way to reach the top of the building and we're set!" said Margot enthusiastically.

The chime on the door announced the presence of an incredibly handsome man, dressed in a bow tie and oversized black glasses. "Who. Is. That?" whispered Margot to Zenna, both enjoying the eye candy.

"Parc!" exclaimed Tali, surprised to see him. "What are you doing here?"

Zenna and Margot exchanged glances – *that* is who Tali had been talking about. They didn't realize that their quiet friend had such good taste in men.

"My boss has me working overtime with a couple of other associates at the firm today," said Parc, glad to be in the presence of Tali again. "I needed a break so I offered to pick us up something to snack on from my favorite bakery in France," he added with a smile. Tali's glow returned to her face, happily boxing up several of her colorful macarons.

"Is that all you need today?" she asked Parc. Parc, who was tempted to offer Tali some sort of cheesy pick-up line ("No actually, I need you") refrained and said, "Yeah I guess that's it for me."

Margot, who was anxious to talk with the attractive Parc, approached him as he was turning away from the counter. "Hey, do you know anywhere that we can get a giant torch? We need it today." Parc tilted his head, amused with the strange question. Then he realized, yes, he actually did know exactly where to get it.

"When do you need it by?" he asked.

"Tonight would be perfect. Meet us here?"

Parc nodded - thrilled that he had a reason to see Tali twice in one day.

"Are we really going to try to do this?" asked Zenna after Parc left. "We're not going to try, we're doing it," Margot smiled. "Tali, can you find your recipe for crème brulee? We're going to need a huge batch."

As Tali and Margot got to work on the custard mixture for their evil plot, Zenna picked up her phone and called Jacques. She relayed the idea for Margot's ridiculous plan to her new boyfriend who laughed hysterically on the other end. "So, you need my help?" Jacques asked, knowing all to well that he was the best when it came to ridiculous. "I think we can make something work," he said, agreeing to meet Zenna and her friends at the bakery later that evening.

Zenna looked at Coty, who was drinking a cup of cocoa and watching a movie on her computer. She had never loved anything more in her whole life and she would do whatever it took to make sure she could keep him.

CRÈME BRULEE

Serves 4

*You will need to multiply the amounts by 150 to cover a large building

INGREDIENTS

- 1 ¾ cups heavy cream
- 1 teaspoon vanilla extract
- 4 egg yolks, cold
- ¼ cup + 4 teaspoons granulated sugar
- 1/8 teaspoon kosher salt
- Special tools
- Mini blowtorch

DIRECTIONS

- Preheat your oven to 300 degrees F. Place 4 six-ounce ramekins in a deep baking dish (one that is as deep or deeper than the ramekins themselves). Boil water in a teakettle.

- In a small saucepan over medium heat bring the cream to a simmer. Take the pan off the heat, cover, and allow the cream to sit for 12 minutes.

- While the cream cools, combine the egg yolks, ¼ cup sugar, and the salt; whisk to combine.
- Use a candy thermometer to check the temperature of the cream. It needs to be below 165 degrees F before continuing. Once the cream is at the right temperature, whisk ½ cup into the egg yolk mixture. Then add the remaining cream and whisk again for 15 seconds. Stir in the vanilla.
- Pour the mixture through a sieve into a large heatproof measuring cup to get rid of any solid bits. Divide the mixture evenly between the 4 ramekins set in the baking pan. The mixture should not come all the way to the top of the ramekins. Carefully pour the hot water from the teakettle into the baking pan, making sure no water gets into the ramekins. The water should come up about 2/3 of the height of the ramekins.
- Place the baking pan with ramekins in your preheated oven and cover with a piece of aluminum foil. Bake the custard for about 45 minutes or until the edges have set and the center is still a bit jiggly, but not liquidy. The custards should not brown in the oven.
- Take the baking pan out of the oven and remove the ramekins from the hot water carefully. Set the ramekins on a wire rack and cool for 30 minutes. Leave uncovered and place in the refrigerator so that they can cool completely. Then cover the ramekins with plastic wrap and refrigerate for at least 3 hours (or up to 2 days).
- Before serving, uncover the ramekins and set on a workspace. Work with one ramekin at a time. Sprinkle a teaspoon of sugar on top of the custard, tapping the sides to even the layer. Turn on the mini torch and hold about 3 inches away from the top of the custard. Moving slowly, move the torch back and forth across the top of the custard. The sugar will melt and turn a deep brown color. The sugar should cool and harden for 2 to 3 minutes before serving.

23

At ten minutes past five the gang reconvened at The Two Macarons. The girls had stayed at the bakery all afternoon preparing exorbitant amounts of custard to paint the walls of the enormous Delroy Doux. Jules was the first of the men to arrive at the bakery, dressed in a black turtleneck and slacks. He had spent his afternoon writing anonymous letters to the press alerting them to a "grand surprise" that was to take place Christmas morning outside the Double D bakery.

Jacques showed up next, calling the girls and Jules to come outside and see what he had found. It turned out that Jacques had a brief stint with a local traveling circus called *Le Plus Fou Des Signes*, where Jacques was known as the craziest of them all. It wasn't enough for him to ride just any old giraffe unicycle while carrying several women on his shoulders – he had to construct one that was nearly four times the size, making it impossible to fit inside the tent, which meant the crowd had to venture outside to see the spectacle of Jacques atop a one-wheeled deathtrap over twelve meters tall.

Jacques gave up his circus days after being given a home in Paris by his grandfather who had passed away, deciding it was time to give up the life of a nomad and settle down, although he still remained eccentric, never having fewer than five jobs and spending many of his days dressed up as animals, mimes, and occasionally women in order to get his fill of fun.

No longer officially part of the *Le Plus Fou* gang, Jacques still had many good friends who were and they were happy to lend him his crazy unicycle for a night, not even bothering to ask him why exactly he needed it knowing all too well that it was going to be for something outrageous.

Jacques leaned the unicycle up against Tali's apartment roof and climbed to the top making it look impossibly easy. "Who wants up?" Jacques shouted down from atop his perch to the amusement of his friends below who were both amazed and afraid at the feat they were witnessing.

"Are we ready?" Jules asked the group, anxious to put his plan to action. "We're still waiting on Parc. Where is he?" Margot asked Tali. Tali was worried that Parc wasn't going to show, that he decided what they were doing was wrong or, worse, that he really wasn't that into her and had found something better to do. "I don't know," Tali replied. "We could start without him."

"No you couldn't," said Parc stepping out of his car, holding a large bag in his hands. Every time he saw Tali he fell for her even more. When she wasn't around, Parc worried that he had exaggerated her beauty and her kindness in his mind. But upon seeing her he realized that his memory wasn't too good to be true. In fact, it wasn't good enough.

"I got it," Parc said, pulling a giant torch out of the brown bag in his hands. Jacques, who had climbed down from his unicycle for the moment, admired the piece of art in Parc's hands. "*La vache!*" Jacques exclaimed. "Where did you find this?"

Apparently Parc's boss, Mr. Palomer, was quite the collector. He loved spending money on ridiculous and rare finds, nothing common like art or even cars; Mr. Palomer loved old machines, ones that functioned but whose function was no longer functional. One such find was the giant torch used to light the Olympic Torch in the 1928 games held in Amsterdam, the first modern Olympics to reintroduce the tradition of the torch. Mr. Palomer paid a pretty penny for this particular piece, nearly half a million Euros. Parc knew all about the torch because he was the one sent to the auction to bid on the piece. Having won it, Parc returned triumphantly to the office to show his boss, who was, surprisingly, less than thrilled. It turned out that Mr. Palomer only enjoyed the thrill of the hunt; enjoying the feast was far too primal for a man of his class. Parc was ordered to drive the torch to Mr. Palomer's home and help one of the guards safely store it in the large warehouse filled with hundreds of rare items, none of which Mr. Palomer cared to look at.

The events of that day put a bad taste in Parc's mouth. He already disliked his boss because he treated other people, including himself, as if they were lesser, which is exactly what they were in Palomer's mind. But after seeing how his money, money that could help others, was carelessly thrown down the drain, Parc detested him.

Which is why today he had no qualms about sneaking into the warehouse at the back of the Palomer estate, distracting the guard dogs with a pear tart tatin he picked up from the bakery, and stealing the torch. Mr. Palomer would never miss it; he would never even know it was gone as Parc planned to return it as soon as it was done being used.

"What exactly are we using the torch for?" Parc asked, the only one still unaware of the plan to crème brulee the competition. The group just smiled.

"Let's go," said Margot, taking Jules by the hand. Jacques helped Zenna on top of his shoulders atop the giant unicycle, the couple taking off ahead of the rest. Tali and Parc trailed behind, not talking, not touching - just enjoying each other's company on this magically strange Christmas Eve.

PEAR TARTE TATIN

Serves 6 (Or 1 pack of hungry dogs)

INGREDIENTS

- 1 cup flour
- ¾ teaspoon kosher salt
- 6 tablespoons unsalted butter, cut into pieces
- 2 tablespoons vegetable shortening
- 3 tablespoons ice water
- For the filling
- 2 ½ pounds pears, peeled, cored, and sliced in half lengthwise
- 1 lemon, for the juice
- 1 ¼ cups granulated sugar
- 6 tablespoons unsalted butter

DIRECTIONS

- Combine the flour and salt in a large mixing bowl. Use your fingers or a pastry blender to add the butter and shortening to the flour mixture. Add the water 1 tablespoon at a time, kneading until it creates dough. Remove the dough ball out of the bowl and wrap in plastic wrap; set in the refrigerator.
- Set your oven's temperature to 425 degrees F. Set the pear halves on a cutting board flat side down. Leaving the stem-end in tact, slice each pear into 4 long slices. Set the pears in a bowl and combine with the lemon juice and ¼ cup of sugar. Allow the filling mixture to set for 20 minutes.
- As the pears set heat the butter in a 9" ovenproof skillet over medium heat. Once the butter melts and in the remaining 1 cup of sugar. Continue cooking until the sugar caramelizes, stirring constantly. Take the skillet off the heat and stir to help it cool.
- Drain the juice off of the pears. Set the pears in the skillet with the browned sugar,

placing the rounded sides down and the stem-ends towards the center. Fan the pear slices by gently pressing on top of each half.

- Remove the dough from the refrigerator and place on a floured work surface. Use a rolling pin to roll the dough into a 10" circle about ¼" thick. Transfer the dough on top of the pears in the skillet, pressing the edge of the dough down inside the skillet to seal the pears in. Remove 4 small pieces of dough from the center of the crust to allow steam to escape. Place the dough-covered skillet in the preheated oven and bake for 25 minutes or until the top of the crust turns golden brown.

- Carefully remove the skillet from the oven. Use a baster to transfer excess juice from the side of the pan into a small saucepan. Heat the juice over high heat until it becomes thick.

- Set a large serving platter on top of the skillet and quickly invert the tart. Spoon the thickened juice over the tops of the pears. Serve the tart warm.

24

December 25th - "*Joyeux Noel!*" Margot announced to Zenna and Coty as they walked into the bakery that morning. Coty was ecstatic, holding a silver robot in his hands, the gift from Pere Noel that he received last night. "Did you see?" Tali asked Zenna coming out from the kitchen to give Coty a Christmas hug. A huge crowd had gathered outside Delroy Doux unable to believe their eyes. A large sign hung over the door that read, "Closed For Repairs." The windows, the doors, the walls were covered in a thick coat of custard and caramelized sugar, making it impossible to open the bakery. Last night's snow had hardened the delectable shell, worsening the situation and infuriating Delroy and Aubin, who were now missing out on what would have been their biggest day since the Sugar Apocalypse.

"So it worked?" smiled Zenna, setting herself down on the floor next to Coty who was in an intense imaginary fight between his new robot and the evil forces presently marching through the front door. Delroy Doux was going to be closed for at least a few days and the huge crowd who gathered outside thanks to a front-page story in the morning's newspaper was growing hungrier by the moment. In anticipation to the mad rush that was seemingly inevitable, the girls double-checked their displays, making sure everything looked perfect; they didn't just need customers today – they needed to win them back for good.

But the crowd didn't come. Peeking out the window Margot saw that the massive group of cold Parisians was starting to disperse, sadly making their way home, forgetting all about the cute bakery that was just a few steps away. "Fuck," muttered Margot, realizing that their grand plan was flawed. Just because DD was closed and tons of people were outside didn't mean they were going to magically remember that there was an even better bakery across the street. "All we did was piss off Paris," Margot said to Zenna, realizing that today really could be their last day in the bakery.

"What's that smell?" asked Zenna who had just caught the scent of sweet cherries and fresh pastry.

"Tali," said Margot, heading to the back with her friend.

"That smells incredible," Margot said to Tali looking over her shoulder at the Cherry Clafoutis she was busy preparing.

"Look!" said Zenna pointing to the air above Tali's head.

The cherries were bursting right before their eyes, each one exploding into thousands of tiny hearts that were floating into the air, filling the kitchen.

"Quick," Margot shouted at Zenna, "open the front doors and let them out. People need to see!"

Zenna ran to the front, leading the charge of millions of cherry-red hearts that danced through the front of the bakery and out into the winter sky. The hearts smelled deliciously ripe, intoxicating the thousands of people making their way home.

"How is this happening?" Zenna asked running back to the kitchen only to see more and more hearts filling the air. "She's in love," said Margot, now finally realizing that true love not only existed, it was more powerful than she ever knew. Margot and Zenna began stirring more batter for the Clafoutis, adding more hearts to the city of Paris, both being madly in love themselves. Coty ran into the kitchen, delighted at the sight. "Mommy!" he exclaimed, "There are a lot of people outside. I think they're hungry." The women gave each other an excited look – this was it.

A line formed outside the bakery and grew all morning and afternoon, as more and more people smelled the love that was flying out of The Two Macarons. Margot, Zenna, and Tali had never seen their bakery so busy. Busy enough, Margot thought, to save the bakery.

As Zenna and Margot tended to the customers in front, Tali was furiously baking in the back. Everything she made that Christmas Day was perfect because her mind was drunk on the thought of Parc. And when food is baked with love there is nothing in the world that can beat the taste and the growing line of people out front were agreeing.

"*Joyeux Noel,*" a voice whispered into Tali's ear, sending goose bumps down her neck. "I just had to see you," said Parc, moving in dangerously close.

"Hi," said Tali shyly, looking up at him from her vulnerable position against the counter. Without another word Parc put his arms around Tali's waist and kissed her. Never in history had there been a kiss so passionate and perfect. Sparks flew wildly throughout the kitchen, igniting small fires on nearby towels and paper bags.

The crowd outside stepped back from the bakery upon hearing loud noises coming from inside. Unable to figure out what was going on, several people in line stepped across the street to get a better view from beneath the Eiffel Tower. Under the legs of tower the small group of people began to see fireworks exploding over the bakery. Upon hearing the exuberant shouts of people across the street, the whole line began to move to see the show. Unbeknownst to the passionate couple in the kitchen, their sparks had turned into fireworks, a display that would last all evening and through the night to the delight of the thousands of people who come to witness the spectacle, and taste the food, that historical Christmas Day.

CHERRY CLAFOUTIS

Serves 8

INGREDIENTS

- 4 eggs, separated
- 2/3 cup granulated sugar
- 6 tablespoons all-purpose flour
- 2 teaspoons pure vanilla extract
- 1 ¼ cup heavy cream
- ½ teaspoon sea salt
- 1 ½ pounds fresh cherries, pitted
- ½ teaspoon freshly grated lemon zest

DIRECTIONS

- Set your oven's temperature to 375 degrees F. Prepare an 8x10" baking dish by buttering; set aside.

- Place the egg yolks and 1/3 cup of the sugar in a large mixing bowl and beat with an electric mixer on medium-high for 6 to 8 minutes or until ribbons begin to form. Next add the flour, vanilla extract, and heavy cream. Adjust your mixer's speed to low and keep beating until everything is well combined.

- In a separate smaller bowl beat the egg whites and salt with a whisk. Pour the beaten egg whites into the batter and beat with the electric mixer on low speed for 1 to 2 minutes.

- Set the empty greased baking dish in the preheated oven for 5 minutes.
- In a clean bowl combine the cherries, remaining 1/3 cup of sugar, and the lemon zest; gently stir to combine. Take the empty pan out of the oven and pour the cherries into the bottom. Cover the cherries with the bottom, smoothing the top with a spatula if necessary. Bake the Clafoutis in the oven for about 30 minutes or until the middle is set.

25

The crowd stayed to watch the fireworks all night, clearing out the bakery of its just-made pastries and desserts every hour. The people were mesmerized by the colorful display and drunken with the love that was exploding from The Two Macarons. So enthralled, the massive group stayed all night in the square under the Eiffel Tower, forming another line in front of the bakery hours before it was scheduled to open, waiting to get their hands on the buttery palmiers Tali and Zenna were busy making in the back.

The love the two were pouring into the palmiers' puff pastry was a million times more powerful than the money that had been poured into Delroy's bakery across the street. Even though Delroy Doux was scheduled to open tomorrow (their crème brulee sabotage not as hard to clean up as they had hoped), the French Hens knew that very few of their old customers would return to the competition's store.

They had gained a powerful following in the last day, the romantics of Paris learning how to once again embrace their indulgent sides. The Two Macarons had become the hot spot in Paris, and the money that they had made in a short 36 hours was plenty to keep Delroy and his new partner in crime, Aubin, at arm's length.

PETIT PALMIERS

Serves 8

INGREDIENTS

- 1 sheet frozen puff pastry
- ½ cup light brown sugar
- 2 tablespoons unsalted butter, melted
- Granulated sugar, for topping

DIRECTIONS

- Carefully unroll the sheet of puff pastry out on a flat work surface. Place a towel over it to keep it moist while thawing until it can be worked with (completely thawed and pliable).

- When the pastry is ready, sprinkle the top with the brown sugar to create a thick layer. Use a rolling pin to press the sugar into the dough more. Tightly roll one edge of the pastry to the center, followed by the opposite edge, making the heart-like palmier shape. Cover the rolled dough in plastic wrap and set in the refrigerator for 25 minutes.

- Set your oven's temperature to 425 degrees F.

- Once the dough is chilled, unwrap and set on the counter. Use a sharp serrated knife to slice the dough into cookies about 1/3" thick. Cover your baking sheets with parchment paper and set the cookies on top leaving 2" of space between each. Use the bottom of a small plate or cup to gently flatten the top of each cookie. Use a pastry brush to brush the top of each with the melted butter, sprinkling a bit of granulated sugar on top. Place the cookies in the preheated oven and bake for about 20 minutes or until they become golden brown.

- Allow the cookies to cool for 10 minutes on the baking sheets before transferring to a wire rack to cool completely.

26

December 26th - The man in the suit returned later that morning, fighting his way through the people that had congregated in front of the bakery, waiting for their turn to taste what all of Paris had been buzzing about. Margot gladly handed him the rent that was due to Mr. Tasse and Mr. Guillory, which he accepted smugly. "Oh," said Margot as the man turned to leave, "Tell Aubin he can fuck himself."

As his mom and her friends were busy tending to the customers that continued to stream through the door, Coty decided it was the perfect time to set his plan to introduce Oralie to his friend Basile, who had been brought to the front of the line earlier so that he could get his seat at his table. Even though the bakery was crowded now, there would always be room for Basile.

Coty saw the old woman and her two grandchildren enter the bakery just moments ago. They were still in line, waiting till it was their turn to place their order. Now was his chance. Now or never, he told himself. Coty snuck behind the counter and took a couple pieces of the Quatre-Quart that was cooling on top. Sneaking along the ground undetected at knee-height, Coty approached Oralie's grandchildren, enticing them to come with him and enjoy a piece of the warm cake that happened to be in his hand.

Happy to bypass the line, Oralie's grandchildren, Aveline and Jasper, followed Coty under a table that was situated just before Basile's. Aveline and Jasper enjoyed their cake, asking Coty all about what he got for Christmas. But Coty, who was focused in carrying out his plan perfectly, didn't answer. He reached out from under the table and grabbed Basile's cane, pulling it in close. Aveline and Jasper had stopped talking; this little boy with the cake was up to something. Curious, they peered out from under the table over Coty's shoulders. Coty was staring intently at the shoes of the people who passed, waiting for a pair of brown riding boots with a looped leather pattern to walk by.

Oralie, who was glad to see that this cute little bakery was finally getting the attention it deserved, realized that her grandchildren were no longer standing by her side. In a panic, she began scanning the bakery for any sign of a little boy in a plaid sweater or a small girl with a silver bow in her hair. But the crowd of adults made it impossible to see anyone shorter than a meter tall. Oralie nicely asked the man behind her to save her spot in line as she began to scour the bakery on foot, checking all the nooks and crannies, notorious for being favorite hiding places for small children.

"Here they come," said Coty to his new friends who were excited to see what this meant. As the boots approached the table they were hiding under Coty thrust the cane between the feet of the owner of the boots, sending her flying through the air and into the lap of a very pleased Basile. Oralie let out a hearty laugh but didn't move to reposition from how she landed. "Hi, I'm Oralie," she said to Basile, placing her arms around his neck. But Basile didn't hear anything – entranced by the golden woman who had fallen from heaven into his lap.

Oralie would spend the rest of her life in that lap, which meant that Basile's table in the corner would never again just be a table for one.

QUATRE-QUART CAKE

Serves 6

INGREDIENTS

- 14 tablespoons salted butter
- 2 ¼ cups self-rising flour
- 1 ¾ cup finely ground sugar
- 3 organic, free-range eggs, separated
- 1 ¼ teaspoon pure vanilla extract

DIRECTIONS

- Set your oven's temperature to 350 degrees F. Boil a teakettle of water. Set an aluminum-roasting pan on the bottom rack of the oven and fill with the boiling water. Shut the door and allow the oven to preheat with the water inside, which will create steam for the cake when it bakes.

- Prepare a 10" round cake pan by greasing and then line with parchment paper; set aside.
- In a mixing bowl combine the butter, vanilla extract, and sugar. Beat with an electric mixer until the butter is creamed and smooth. Place the egg yolks in a small bowl and the egg whites in another small bowl. Use the electric mixer to beat the yolks and a wire whisk to beat the whites until they are stiff.
- Add the egg yolks to the butter mixture, adding a couple tablespoons of the flour, and mix until combined. In batches add the remaining flour, mixing until combined. Then fold in the egg whites with a spatula.
- Pour the batter into the prepared cake pan and place into the preheated oven with the tray of water still on the bottom rack. Bake the cake for about 40 minutes or until the top of the cake becomes golden and a toothpick inserted into the center comes out clean. Do your best to resist opening the door of the oven until at least 30 minutes have passed so that the cake won't sink in the middle.
- The cake should cool on a wire rack for at least 20 minutes before slicing and enjoying.

27

December 27th - With the bakery saved from eminent closure, the Three French Hens finally had a day to enjoy. Their bakery was busy, their boyfriends were close, and Coty was happily playing with Aveline and Jasper who had come in with their grandma and Basile just a few moments ago. Margot looked at the scene from behind the counter and realized that she was happy. Despite her wavering in deciding whether or not to keep The Two Macarons, or even save it for that matter, she had come to the decision that she would stay at the bakery for a while longer. She wasn't a natural business woman, didn't love baking like Zenna, and wasn't even super talented at it like Tali, but she did love knowing that her little corner of Paris brought people together, just like it had brought her and Jules together only days before.

Jules, who was writing at a nearby table, caught Margot's eyes, his head gesturing for her to come over and keep him company. Margot slinked over to Jules's table, leaving Zenna in the front to handle the customers, which she was completely capable of doing. Zenna had a way of commanding the room with just a look, something Margot was sure she picked up in her years living on the streets and fending for herself.

With Margot and Zenna distracted, a visitor snuck past the line and into the kitchen, glad to see that Tali's friends were oblivious to his presence, giving him the perfect opportunity to finally finish his romp in the hen house.

Tali was busy wiping down the surface of one of the large counters in the kitchen, preparing a clean work surface for her next batch of dough. Although she was swamped with work, she didn't mind, her mind free of the constraints of time; its only thought was when she would see Parc again. "There you are," said a deep voice from behind her. The man was admiring her firm ass, her body as perfect as he had remembered. She had been on his "to-do" list for a long time, and considering that he now owned her building, he felt like she was even more like his property, which made his next action even more justifiable in his mind.

Aubin approached Tali, surprising her with his presence as she was expecting to see Parc.

"What are you doing back here?" Tali asked looking around hoping that Margot or Zenna would walk in any moment.

"You," Aubin replied, sliding his hand up her skirt, feeling around the edges of her lace panties.

Tali tried to move his hand away but he was too strong. He set his free hand on the counter behind her and leaned in, pressing against her chest and breathing heavily on her neck. Tali wanted to yell for help but was paralyzed, afraid of what was going to happen next.

"Get the fuck off of her you douche," Zenna screamed. She had walked to the back to reload an empty tray with a fresh batch of napoleons, which were flying off the shelves this morning.

"Zenna," said Aubin laughing. He moved off of Tali and began to walk away, but as he did he turned back to her and said, "Don't worry, I'll have you when I want."

As Aubin made his way out of the kitchen, he grabbed one of the napoleons off a tray on the cart near the door. Apparently Aubin felt like he didn't need to ask for permission for anything, including sex, anymore. Now in cahoots with Delroy Tasse, Aubin felt omnipotent.

"What if he comes back?" Tali cried into Zenna's shoulder.

"He won't," she replied, not just to comfort her friend but because she knew that she had done something that would solve the Aubin problem for good.

On Christmas Eve, while the girls were plotting to sabotage Delroy Doux, Zenna decided to come up with a back-up plan, desperate to make sure that she would never have to worry about losing custody to her son. She had asked Jacques, who she realized would do anything for her, to pick her up a few sticks of highly explosive dynamite, knowing that he of all people would know exactly where to find it and, more importantly, wouldn't ask questions. Had the crème brulee plan failed, Zenna was prepared to do something much more damaging, blowing up the competition literally.

Thankfully it hadn't come to this, but Zenna still had the dynamite, unsure of how to safely dispose of it. She had stashed it at her home for a night, but was afraid that Coty would get his hands on it. This morning she had arranged to have Jacques pick it up from The Two Macarons and take it back to wherever he got it from. All morning she had been walking, slowly and methodically, through the bakery with an apron filled with dynamite.

The sight of Aubin made Zenna physically sick. She couldn't believe that he had the balls to assault Tali right there in the kitchen, with the woman he screwed and the woman whose heart he trampled right out front. She wanted to kill Aubin. Without thinking, Zenna quickly slipped a stick of dynamite into one of the napoleons before confronting Aubin. She had gotten to know Aubin well while he dated Margot and she knew that he wouldn't be able to resist a fresh napoleon, taking one as he left to emphasize that he absolutely had no respect for the women or their bakery.

Screams filled the air less than twenty seconds after Aubin walked out the front door of The Two Macarons. The media reported later that a man, who would later be identified as Mr. Aubin Guillory by his wallet found nearly fifty meters away by investigators, the wealthy entrepreneur and heir to the Guillory fortune, had exploded in front of the Eiffel Tower. It wasn't spontaneous combustion, as some witnesses swore, but murder and the police swore they wouldn't rest until the criminal was found.

NAPOLEONS

Serves 9

INGREDIENTS

- 1 sheet frozen puff pastry, thawed
- For the filling
- ¼ cup granulated sugar
- 2 tablespoons all-purpose flour
- Pinch of sea salt
- 1 cup half and half
- 2 egg yolks, lightly beaten
- ½ teaspoon pure vanilla extract
- ¼ cup whipping cream
- ***Dynamite not recommended***
- For the glaze
- 2 cups powdered sugar, sifted
- ¼ teaspoon almond extract
- 2 ½ tablespoons water, boiling
- For the chocolate drizzle
- 1 ½ tablespoons melted semisweet chocolate

DIRECTIONS

- Set your oven's temperature to 425 degrees F. Prepare 2 baking sheets by lining with parchment paper; set aside.
- Unroll the puff pastry and trim to a 9" square. Use a knife to cut the square into 9 three-inch squares. Place the squares onto the lined baking sheets and prick the tops with the tines of a fork. Set the pastry squares in the preheated oven and bake for about 20 minutes or until they are golden in color. When finished baking, remove from the parchment paper and place on a wire rack to cool.
- Next prepare the cream filling by combining the sugar, flour, and salt together in a medium-size saucepan – stir to combine. Then add in the half and half, stirring over medium heat. The mixture should start to bubble and get thick. Continue stirring and cook for another minute.
- Place the beaten eggs in a bowl and add half of the hot half and half mixture, stirring to combine. Pour this mixture back into the remaining half and half mixture in the saucepan, stirring and cooking for another 2 minutes. Take the saucepan off the heat and add the vanilla extract. Pour the mixture into a bowl and cover with plastic wrap. Allow the mixture to cool until warm. When warm, in a small mixing bowl use an electric mixer to beat the whipping cream until it holds soft peaks. Use a spatula to gently fold the whipped cream into the warm filling.
- Finally prepare the glaze by combining the powdered sugar and almond extract in a medium-size mixing bowl. Slowly add the boiling water, stirring until it reaches a consistency that will be easy to spread.
- To put the napoleons together, use a fork to carefully separate each baked puff pastry square into 3 layers. Place 1 to 2 tablespoons of the filling on each bottom layer of pastry. Set the second layer of pastry on top and place another 1 to 2 tablespoons of filling on top of that. Set the final pastry layer on top, spreading the glaze in an even layer. Use a dull knife to drizzle the melted chocolate on top.
- Enjoy the napoleons immediately or place in the refrigerator for up to 12 hours. (The sooner you eat them the better!)

28

December 28th - After seeing the area around The Two Macarons swarmed with police activity – detectives, horses, bloodhounds – Zenna knew she would be caught. It was just a matter of time. She hadn't thought her plan through. In fact it wasn't a plan at all. Tali and Margot weren't sure that Zenna had committed the crime, but they thought that she was definitely a prime suspect. Plus, Zenna had been acting nervous all day, spending more time than usual in the back of the bakery, asking Coty to come with her wherever she went, and on the phone with Jacques every other minute.

At around noon that day three police officers walked into the bakery, asking Basile and Oralie if they knew whom the owner was. The couple described Margot, saying that they believed she was in the back at this very moment. Thankfully, the police officers didn't need to go to the back themselves as Margot walked out the kitchen door at that very moment. The officers sat her down at a table that had been moved away into a back corner, asking her all sorts of questions about Aubin. Although Margot knew she had nothing to do with Aubin's death, she was nervous that they could make a case against her, saying that she had a motive – the mad ex-girlfriend seeking revenge against her cheating boyfriend that had recently bought the building her business was in.

"May we interview your employees?" the officers asked Margot after finishing her initial interview.

"Sure," said Margot, doing her best to remain calm.

While in view of the officers she walked slowly to the back, but as soon as she hit the corner she began to run.

"The police want to interview you both," she said shaking. "I think they suspect one of us murdered Aubin."

Zenna placed her hands over Coty's ears, "I did," she whispered.

Stunned that their friend could actually kill someone, Margot and Tali were left without a word to say. But knowing they needed to act quickly, Margot sprang into action. "Tali, you go out now and buy some time for Zenna. Give her the keys to your apartment so she has a place to hide."

Tali reached into her pocket and handed Zenna, who was now bawling, her keys. "Go Tali," Margot insisted. Tali looked back at Zenna and Coty with as much of a smile as she could muster, knowing very well that this might be the last time she ever saw them both.

While Tali obligingly answered the questions, being as talkative as a shy person like herself could manage, Margot helped Zenna and Coty sneak into the small room that was Tali's home.

"What am I going to do?" cried Zenna, no longer able to keep it together for the sake of her son.

"Call Jacques."

Zenna reached out her phone but was shaking so hard that she was unable to dial his number.

"Can you?" she asked her friend.

"Jacques?" said Margot, covering the speaker of the phone with her cupped hand to muffle her voice.

"It's Margot. Zenna and Coty need your help. It's serious. We're in Tali's apartment next to the bakery. Hurry, please."

Margot hung up, nervously peeking out the window, waiting to see what Jacques would have up his sleeve.

Like magic, Jacques appeared within seconds. He was flying in an old hot air balloon, decorated with blue and green flags. He stood in the wood basket wearing a fur trapper hat and goggles. He pulled the balloon up to the window, spotting Margot.

"Are my passengers ready for their flight?" he shouted to her.

Margot motioned for Zenna and Coty to come to the window, pulling a chair up next to it to help them climb into the floating basket. Jacques held his hand out for Coty, who got in first, and then helped Zenna in.

"Your chariot awaits my darling," he said, knowing that this would be the first day of the rest of their lives.

Waving to her best friend as they pulled away from the window, Margot spotted a bag of Madeleines on the table. She tossed it out the window.

"For the road!"

Zenna caught the butter cakes and blew Margot a kiss with tears of every emotion streaming down her face.

It wasn't the last time Margot saw Zenna, Jacques, and Coty, but it would be another fifty years before she did. Jacques flew his criminal and her son to a small island off the coast of Denmark, somewhere between Copenhagen and Gothenburg. There he married Zenna in a small church with only the minister and Coty as witnesses. Jacques made money fishing and entertaining the fisherman who docked on their small island. He and Zenna had three more children, giving Coty plenty of playmates to romp with on their twenty-acre farm. It took decades for Zenna to have the courage to contact Margot, finding her name mentioned in a small article in a Swedish newspaper, the wife of the author of the currently hottest book on the market. When the two reunited, they laughed at how old they had gotten. And then, settling in on Zenna's front porch, they picked up right where they left off, talking about love, sex, and clothes like they were in their twenties again.

MADELEINES

Serves 12

INGREDIENTS

- 2 fresh eggs
- ¾ teaspoon almond extract
- 1/8 teaspoon kosher salt
- 1/3 cup granulated sugar
- ½ cup all-purpose flour
- 1 ½ tablespoons freshly grated lemon zest
- ¼ cup unsalted butter, melted and cooled to room temperature
- Granulated sugar, for topping
- Special tools
- Madeleine molds

DIRECTIONS

- Set your oven's temperature to 375 degrees F. Prepare your Madeleine molds by buttering and flouring 12; set aside.

- Place the eggs and vanilla in a small mixing bowl and beat with an electric mixer on high speed until the eggs become light. Continue beating as you add the sugar in batches. Keep beating on high speed for another 6 to 8 minutes, working until the mixture thickens and ribbons form when the beaters are lifted out of the batter.

- In 3 batches add the flour into the batter, using a spatula to fold in after each addition. Then add the lemon zest and melted butter, folding in gently but quickly. Use a large spoon to transfer the batter into the prepared molds, mounding it just over the tops.

- Place the filled molds in the preheated oven and bake for about 15 minutes or until the tops of the cakes become springy to the touch. When finished baking, use a knife to loosen the Madeleines from the sides of the pan. Place the Madeleines on a wire cooling rack and sprinkle with sugar while still warm.

29

December 31st - Tali stretched her arms as she woke up, looking out the window to a giant terrace overlooking the Seine. It was better than she had ever pictured in her dreams. Looking over at Parc, who was still asleep beneath the white cotton sheets, she smiled. He was the man of her dreams, the true love she had been waiting for. The night before, as her and Parc were walking hand-in-hand through the tree-lined path in front of the Champs-Elysees, Tali felt the presence of her mom and dad. Looking over her shoulder, she could have sworn she saw them walking behind her, hand-in-hand. Tali took it as a sign that her parents approved of Parc and that he was, indeed, *the one*. She and Parc walked all over Paris that night, ending up at the door of Parc's apartment for the very first time.

"It's not much," he said as he opened the door, "but someday soon I'll be able to buy a bigger place for us... for me," he corrected, not sure if it was okay to say something like that so soon. As Tali walked through the front door her eyes went directly to the French doors that lead out onto a terrace, a terrace where she would paint the landscape below for years to come.

Parc met Tali out on the terrace with a bottle of champagne, letting the cork fly over the edge and into the night sky. They clinked their glasses and leaned over the ledge counting the stars together in silence.

"I've dreamt of this moment for years," said Parc, deciding that he couldn't keep his feelings for Tali to himself anymore.

"You have too?" said Tali, studying Parc's face, happy to see that he was doing the same with hers.

"I've seen your face for years, whenever I close my eyes, but I was starting to think you didn't exist."

Tali's smile made Parc's eyes light up. He went in for a kiss.

Tali, who was leaning in too, knocked her glass of champagne off the ledge with her elbow, sending the glass tumbling through the air and into the river below. As Tali and Parc kissed, the people of Paris enjoyed a river of champagne that flowed for hours, the entire city coming to the river's edge, dipping in their glasses, and toasting to the generous couple on the terrace above.

Looking over now at Parc on New Year's Eve morning, Tali decided to surprise him with a special treat for breakfast. Slipping on a blue button-down shirt of his, Tali snuck into the kitchen and began making the dough for one of her favorite desserts, chocolate frosted éclairs.

Tali put the finishing touches on, smoothing her knife over the freshly made frosting. She set the éclairs on a tray and began to carry them towards the bedroom, but Parc was already up, coming into the living room in nothing but tight gray briefs.

"I thought you left," he said, happy to see that he was wrong.

"Leave?" said Tali, unable to imagine why a girl would leave a man like Parc without being forced. "I can't leave until you taste these," she said, setting the tray of éclairs down on the coffee table in front of his sofa. Parc sat down next to her, amazed that she could make such an incredible breakfast in such a short amount of time.

Looking at Tali this morning Parc decided that he never wanted her to leave and decided to tell her so. Tali, who knew this moment was inevitable, threw her arms around Parc, showing him, rather than telling him, that she agreed. They made love again that morning and then feasted on the éclairs.

The chocolate frosted éclairs quickly became a favorite weekend treat in the home of Parc and Tali, enjoying them nearly every weekend, sharing them with family who came to visit, children who woke up early on Sundays to watch TV, and, of course, with each other. Before Parc's final day on earth, he would have enjoyed Tali's éclairs exactly 3,642 times. And when the met in heaven again, Tali made sure that the tradition continued, her only request to God at the gates of heaven that she have her ingredients, a kitchen, and her beloved Parc to share them with.

CHOCOLATE FROSTED ÉCLAIRS

Serves 12

INGREDIENTS

- 1 cup cold water
- 8 tablespoons unsalted butter
- 2 tablespoons granulated sugar
- ¼ teaspoon salt
- 1 cup + 3 tablespoons all-purpose flour
- 4 large brown eggs
- For the filling
- 2 cups whole milk
- 1 teaspoon vanilla extract
- ½ cup + 2 tablespoons granulated sugar
- 5 tablespoons cake flour
- 1/8 teaspoon kosher salt
- 1 large brown egg
- 2 large egg yolks
- ¼ cup + 2 tablespoons heavy cream
- For the glaze
- 4 ounces bittersweet chocolate, melted
- 4 tablespoons unsalted butter, softened

DIRECTIONS

- Set your oven's temperature to 400 degrees F.

- Place the water, butter, sugar, and salt in a medium saucepan over medium heat; bring to a boil. Take the pan off the heat and add in the flour, stirring quickly with a wooden spoon for 2 to 3 minutes until a dough forms. Place the dough in a large bowl and beat with an electric mixer on medium for 1 minute. Then, one at a time, add in the eggs, beating well after each.

- Place the dough in a large pastry bag with a round tip, about 1". Use the bag to pipe 12 long logs, about 5" long, onto a baking sheet. Set the baking sheet in the preheated oven and bake for 10 minutes. Reduce the oven's temperature to 325 degrees F. and bake the éclair shells for another 30 minutes or until they are golden brown in color. Place the baked shells on a wire rack to cool.

- Place the milk for the filling in a medium saucepan and bring to a boil.
- While waiting for the milk to boil, combine the sugar, cake flour, and salt in a large bowl and whisk to combine. Then whisk in the egg and egg yolks. Once the milk is hot, slowly add to the bowl, whisking to combine. Add the vanilla extract. Pour the mixture back into the saucepan and heat over medium – continue whisking. Bring the filling back to a boil, whisking for another 30 seconds until thick. Strain the filling through a sieve into a medium-size bowl and then cover with plastic wrap. Set the filling in the refrigerator to cool for 30 minutes to 1 hour.
- Place the heavy cream in a medium bowl and whip with an electric mixer until it holds soft peaks. Take the filling out of the refrigerator and whisk. Then fold in the whipped cream.
- Combine the melted chocolate with the butter in a medium bowl, stirring until smooth.
- Use a sharp serrated knife to split the cooled shell in half lengthwise. Place a large amount of the filling into the bottom of each. Dip or pour the glaze onto the top portions of the shells before placing on top of the cream-filled bottom.

30

Margot and Jules celebrated New Year's Eve in the kitchen of The Two Macarons, sipping champagne between kisses and conversation.

"Well, you did it," said Jules, toasting Margot.

"We did it," she said correcting him. "I don't know what I would have done without you. You really are my knight in shining armor."

Margot laughed after saying this, recognizing how silly it sounded coming from the mouth of a grown woman.

But it was true. Jules had rescued Margot from a very dark place, somewhere much worse than any dungeon she could remember from the stories her father read to her as a little girl. Margot really believed that she could spend the rest of her life with Jules. He was the kind of man every woman wanted, but too afraid to look for. She was done with meaningless sex, but, looking at Jules leaning against the door of the oven, she realized not done with good sex. Not ever, but especially not tonight.

"Do you want to know what happens next in this story?" Jules asked her, taking another sip from his glass.

"I think I already know," she said as she unbuttoned his pants and slid them down to the floor.

Margot pulled Jules's shirt over his head, realizing that despite all of the sex she had over the last several months she had never had a naked man in her kitchen. She was glad – the bakery maybe the one sacred place left in all of Paris. Margot reached her arms above her head, allowing Jules to lift her shirt off. He unhooked her bra and caressed her breasts while he kissed her neck and collarbone.

They made love for the first time on a bed of pastries, their sweat mixing furiously with the sugar below.

Exhausted but ecstatic, Margot collapsed on Jules's bare chest. Jules, wanting to add his writer's perspective to the situation opened his mouth, only to be stopped mid-sentence by a spoonful of chocolate soufflé Margot had magically just pulled out of the oven. His mouth full of warm soufflé, Margot covered it with her finger before he could try to speak again. "I know how this story is going to end too," she said grinning. "But right now, let's just enjoy the chapter."

Resting naked in Jules's arms on the floor of her bakery Margot realized that heaven must be mind-blowing if it can beat this – lovers in a bakery.

CHOCOLATE SOUFFLÉ

Serves 8

INGREDIENTS

- 5 tablespoons unsalted butter
- 12 ounces bittersweet chocolate, chopped
- 9 large egg yolks
- ½ cup + 2 tablespoons granulated sugar
- 3 large egg whites

DIRECTIONS

- Set your oven's temperature to 350 degrees F. Butter a 5-cup soufflé dish or 8 individual dishes and dust with flour.

- Over very low heat, melt the chocolate and butter in a large saucepan, stirring constantly.

- In a large bowl, beat the egg yolks with ½ cup of sugar for 4 minutes or until the mixture thickens and lightens in color. Use a spatula to fold in the melted chocolate and butter mixture.

- In a clean mixing bowl, beat the egg whites on high speed until they hold soft peaks. Add the remaining 2 tablespoons of sugar a little at a time, beating for another minute. Use a spatula to fold the egg whites into the chocolate mixture and then transfer into the prepare dish/dishes.
- Bake the soufflé in the preheated oven for about 25 minutes or until the soufflé rises and cracks. When finished, the center should still be a bit jiggly. Serve immediately.

Discover More Great Books At
WWW.LITTLEPEARLPUBLISHING.COM